To our families

Practicum in Adapted Physical Activity

Claudia Emes, PhD
The University of Calgary

Beth P. Velde, PhD
East Carolina University

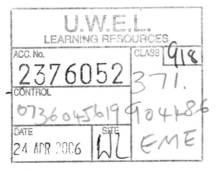

Human Kinetics

Library of Congress Cataloging-in-Publication Data

Emes, Claudia, 1946-
  Practicum in adapted physical activity / Claudia Emes, Beth Velde.
     p. cm.
  Includes bibliographical references.
  ISBN 0-7360-4561-9 (soft cover)
  1. Physical education for people with disabilities. I. Velde, Beth P. II. Title.
  GV445.E64 2004
  371.9'04486--dc22

                              2004008986

ISBN: 0-7360-4561-9

The Web addresses cited in this text were current as of June 2004, unless otherwise noted.

Acquisitions Editor: Bonnie Pettifor; **Developmental Editor:** Jennifer Clark; **Assistant Editor:** Derek Campbell; **Copyeditor:** John Wentworth; **Proofreader:** Anne Rogers; **Permission Manager:** Dalene Reeder; **Graphic Designer:** Fred Starbird; **Graphic Artist:** Dawn Sills; **Photo Manager:** Kareema McLendon; **Cover Designer:** Keith Blomberg; **Photographer (cover):** Claudia Emes; **Photographer (interior):** Claudia Emes, except where otherwise noted. Photo on p. 127 © Rotary Challenger Park; **Art Manager:** Kelly Hendren; **Illustrators:** Kelly Hendren and Kareema McLendon; **Printer:** United Graphics

Printed in the United States of America   10   9   8   7   6   5   4   3   2   1

Human Kinetics
Web site: www.HumanKinetics.com

United States: Human Kinetics
P.O. Box 5076
Champaign, IL 61825-5076
800-747-4457
e-mail: humank@hkusa.com

Canada: Human Kinetics
475 Devonshire Road Unit 100
Windsor, ON N8Y 2L5
800-465-7301 (in Canada only)
e-mail: orders@hkcanada.com

Europe: Human Kinetics
107 Bradford Road
Stanningley
Leeds LS28 6AT, United Kingdom
+44 (0) 113 255 5665
e-mail: hk@hkeurope.com

Australia: Human Kinetics
57A Price Avenue
Lower Mitcham, South Australia 5062
08 8277 1555
e-mail: liaw@hkaustralia.com

New Zealand: Human Kinetics
Division of Sports Distributors
NZ Ltd.
P.O. Box 300 226 Albany
North Shore City
Auckland
0064 9 448 1207
e-mail: blairc@hknewz.com

Contents

Preface

Welcome to the world of service delivery in adapted physical activity (APA). This manual provides you with guidelines and exercises to assist you in growing as a person and help you have a successful practicum experience. Your practicum—which means simply "a context for practice"—is your opportunity to apply your skills of service delivery in APA in an authentic situation. Adapted physical activity practica vary from student to student and, depending on the location of the placement, from setting to setting; each practicum placement provides a unique experience. We believe that experiential learning is critical to deeper understanding and appreciation of adapted physical activity. With that in mind, we designed this manual to further promote your learning experience. It is meant to guide and focus your learning during your practical experience.

This manual is designed to

- supplement the textbook and other recommended reading in your APA course,
- help you grow and develop as a practitioner and assist you in improving your service delivery skills in adapted physical activity practicum,
- support the most memorable experience of your learning journey,
- give you opportunities to participate in exercises and activities directly relevant to your practicum,
- promote the understanding of your choices of professional behaviors,
- aid in your reflection on your practicum experience through journal writing, self-assessment, and critical reflective thinking, and
- guide you through the phases of preparing for, participating in, and evaluating your practicum learning experience.

Regardless of your practicum setting, you'll face ethical considerations, social issues, and safety concerns that will enrich your experience and teach you valuable lessons. This manual helps you make well-considered decisions. Many students report that their practicum is the best part of the course. This book was written with that goal in mind.

We can narrow our primary objectives for this book to these three:

1. To assist you in using your unique skills or knowledge in the practicum situation. This is a learning situation for you, but you have much to offer; one objective of the learning exercises and reflective journaling is to help develop your confidence in your role as a practicum student. We want you to be confident in your abilities and anxious to use your unique skills.

2. To help you learn more about service delivery by integrating theoretical classroom learning with the learning exercises in this book and using new approaches to serving people with disability in APA by applying the principles described in the workbook.

3. To provide you with your own written record of the learning and growth you have experienced during your practicum. The learning exercises and your reflective journaling are your personal record of the success you enjoy in your practicum. This record is not just a keepsake but a reference for your decision-making and future planning in APA.

How to Use This Book Most Effectively During Your Practicum

Being an active learner means that you'll use your practicum as an opportunity to apply the knowledge and skills you bring with you as well as the new knowledge and skills you acquire in your APA course or program. This manual focuses on three kinds of professional practice that come into play during each phase of your practicum: preparation, participation, and evaluation. We suggest that you complete the exercises with your individual practicum placement in mind. There are times when your placement might not be a "good fit" to a learning exercise. In such a case, you might adopt a hypothetical situation to complete the exercise—they usually fit perfectly. But life doesn't work that way, nor will your future practice in APA. Remember that this workbook is part of a learning experience; the learning exercises are not about right and wrong answers—they're about critical thinking and decision making. They are also an opportunity to explore new ideas.

Reflective journaling is a personal learning exercise. Although collaboration and cooperative exercises are an important part of learning, journaling requires that you turn to yourself and reflect on your own personal experience. Journaling is a chance for you to record your personal feelings, perspectives, and emotions. Celebrate your triumphs in writing, as well as noting your challenges, failures, and disappointments—they're all important contributors to learning. Your journal entries will reflect your personal journey, which can change along the way, so your entries might vary in tone and content over the duration of your practicum. Review your entries from time to time and consider if and how your behaviors and reactions have transformed. Look for recurring themes, or try to build a sense of development that might be reflected in your journal.

The learning exercises in this book should coincide with the phases of your practicum. Some exercises are most helpful before participating in your practicum, and others are designed to reflect on your experience during your practicum.

The context of this book is grounded in an abilities-based approach to APA. The information you find here supports participation in practica from several different perspectives but also addresses the tools for abilities-based service delivery.

Part I—Setting the Stage: Preparation

Part I is foundational to the rest of the book and the practicum experience. It sets the stage by defining the practicum in terms of placement, processes, and responsibilities that students will encounter. This part introduces tools for successfully establishing a practicum and builds fundamental philosophical considerations that influence service delivery in APA. Part I concludes with inclusive teaming, a popular approach to delivering programs in APA.

Part II—Getting Into It: Participation

In part II, the considerations associated with working at a placement are addressed, including supervision of the practicum student, learning plans and their implementation, and assessment tools. Students in a practicum that occurs at a different location each week will find this section useful by applying the exercises to a single session. There's also an issue regarding the variety of supervised settings and unsupervised practica. Where appropriate, the exercises could be completed with the course instructor being viewed as the supervisor. Relating to supervisors within a practicum might present a set of challenges to students. Learning about the purposes of supervision and the impact and responsibilities that go along with it can help you understand the relationship that you develop with your supervisor.

After learning about the role of supervision in the practicum, you'll have a clearer understanding about your role. To clarify your understanding further, we'll guide you in creating learning objectives for yourself (chapter 6). This leads to developing a learning plan and recognizing how your needs coincide with the program's objectives. This chapter is designed to clarify the expectations of everyone involved in the practicum, including the host of the program, the supervisor, the participants, and you.

Part II concludes with assessment skills, which are used in the abilities-based approach to evaluate the functional abilities required by an activity within six categories: mobility, object manipulation, cognitive function, communication and perception, behavior and social skills, and fitness. To maximize opportunities for successful participation, the "compatibility overlap" between the abilities required by the activity and the abilities of the individual should be maximized. The processes to assess and improve compatibility overlap are explored in this section.

Part III—Looking Back: Evaluation

Your study of part III should coincide with the end of your practicum. This part is devoted to reviewing and reflecting on what you've learned and what new skills you've acquired. You're encouraged to identify the personal outcomes of your practicum experience. There are exercises to help you create a constructive evaluation on both the program and its participants.

The last chapter of part III focuses on leaving your practicum. There's a lot to reflect back on when you're leaving a placement, and there are also things to take care of before the end of the final session. The way you leave your practicum is as important as the way you begin it.

Finally, there's an opportunity for more reflection. This time you'll be asked to describe the lessons you learned during the practicum. Here we're referring to the many unplanned "learnings" that don't fit under a goal or an objective and that aren't part of the evaluation process. Here's an example from Kevin's journal: "I've noticed that aside from helping with the actual physical exercise, some of the most helpful things I can do is to be supportive and try to make each day that I am here as positive as possible."

Appendix: Journal Writing Guidelines

The appendix includes an area for your journal writing. Your journal is as personal as a diary. Through reflective writing, it brings together the knowledge you're acquiring in class with the experience of your practicum, adding a personal dimension to your learning.

Part 1

SETTING THE STAGE:
Preparation

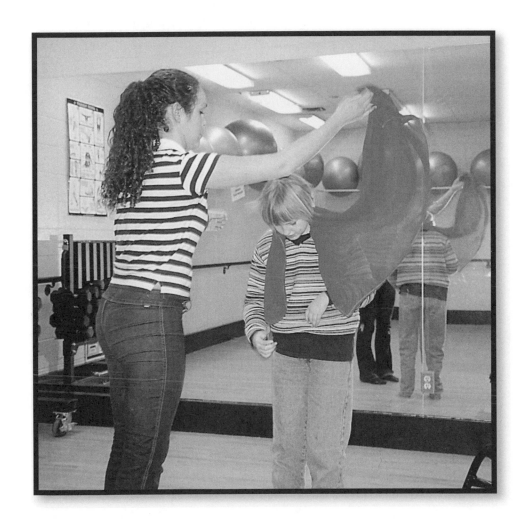

"Experience teaches only the teachable."

Aldous Huxley (1894–1963)

1

Learning Service Delivery

"Self-confidence is the first requisite to great undertakings."

Samuel Johnson (1709–1784)

When Nadia and Ashley discussed the first class of their adapted physical activity course, they shared their anticipation as well as some apprehension. Ashley said, "What do you think about the practicum where we'll work with someone with a disability? I've never done that before." With soccer practice every day after school and her part-time work on Saturdays, she had never found time to volunteer. When she got to college she had continued in competitive sports and spent her other hours either studying or working when she was not attending class.

After high school, Nadia started volunteering three times a week as an assistant soccer coach and also volunteered as a Sunday school teacher at her church. Despite this leadership experience, she was nervous about starting a practicum because, like Ashley, she had no personal experience in working with someone with a disability.

The uncertainty that Nadia and Ashley felt is very natural. Facing a new situation is always a little unnerving. Not knowing what you'll have to do and wondering what will be different and how you'll get started are quite reasonable concerns. Feeling that you're not prepared or experienced enough to take on this kind of responsibility is also understandable.

Perhaps you have experience working with people with disabilities in an activity setting. Maybe you were a volunteer with Special Olympics or in a high school volunteer program in which you had the opportunity to work with and get to know someone with a disability. If so, these valuable experiences have surely enriched your life. Your practicum will be a different kind of experience. In your practicum you'll be linking classroom knowledge to "hands-on" experience working with people who have the disabilities you'll be studying.

Or possibly you're like Nadia and Ashley, and this will be your first experience working with someone who has a disability. If so, after some time, you'll learn to apply classroom knowledge to your experience. Also important—your practicum will help you *learn about yourself* as you're learning about the abilities of others.

What Is a Practicum?

A practicum is an opportunity to apply the knowledge and skills you're acquiring in your adapted physical activity (APA) course. You get to practice professional skills in a supportive learning environment. Your classroom learning in your APA course and your other courses focus on your growth as a professional. Your practicum will include written exercises and journaling to help you think critically and constructively about your APA experience.

The APA Practicum

Although you might be participating in a practicum placement side by side with other APA students, each student's practicum will be unique. The interactions between you and those with whom you work create individual experiences and learning. Of course, in many cases, practica will vary considerably because the location, type of program, and responsibilities of practicum students will vary. We begin this section by exploring the various possibilities for practicum placement.

Practicum Supervisory Formats

You might be working in a practicum setting without direct supervision. In these programs you might be asked to pitch in with very little support or assistance from another person associated with the program. Or you might work under the supervision of someone in the APA program who is an instructor, coach, therapist, or volunteer. In these programs your responsibilities will likely be related to program goals and objectives established before you entered the scene.

If you're in a supervised situation, the expectations of your supervisor could follow several formats. For example, in a program of inclusive physical education the teacher might request that you focus on promoting certain communication behaviors for a young student who has autism. Your job might be to reinforce appropriate communication that is currently the focus not just in physical education but in the classroom and home environments as well. The supervisor identifies certain areas of responsibility for you that guide your practicum activities, but there will probably be other things to do in the practicum that aren't spelled out so clearly.

In other supervised practica the directions you receive might be more vague. For example, in an inclusive swim program, the supervisor might request that you work with a swimmer who has severe cerebral palsy. You might be wondering, Is that all the direction I'm going to get? You might not be exactly sure what's expected of you. Well, the likely expectation in this case is for you to determine the abilities of the swimmer and work toward improving his or her capabilities in a way that is parallel to and consistent with the rest of the class. But don't take our word for it. When the instructions that you receive are vague, ask questions. At the end of the class, ask others about your performance, get feedback from the supervisor on how you did, and be sure to ask the person you're working with about your performance.

In a semisupervised situation, you might be working with someone who won't be immediately present in every situation. You might be asked to take a leadership role in designing and delivering a program. If so, your work will probably require the approval of a supervisor or a senior volunteer within the program. Engage in frequent conversations to ensure that this person has a strong sense for monitoring the progress of the program and your practicum.

Supervisors are usually paid staff, but it's possible a volunteer could supervise you. If so, be sure to establish lines of communication and ensure that this person is willing to spend the time it takes to supervise a practicum student. Although writing a contract isn't usually necessary, you should be very clear about each other's responsibilities. Regardless of the background of your supervisor, get to know him or her and learn about the expectations and goals within the program. Whenever possible, learn from your supervisor's experience.

In an unsupervised situation, *you never know what's possible until you try.* It's not unusual to end up in a practicum with little or no direct supervision. For example, in a community-based after-school program, Jillian was asked to work with Mia, a young girl in a wheelchair. Mia arrived at the center via special transportation (a handi-bus) that always dropped her off after the other children had arrived. Jillian would meet Mia at the bus and take her for a snack; then they would go to a spare room for some one-on-one skill-development time before joining the other children, who were playing in the gym. It was Jillian's responsibility to find activities to share with Mia during one on one and to manage their shared experience. She then helped the leader with games and activities in the gym. Jillian had no direct supervision and she had to choose what to do.

Practicum Settings

If this is your first practicum placement, you might not realize all the possible settings for APA practica. In the community, numerous opportunities exist for a practicum placement: in-home programs of exercise therapy, personal training, or activity partner as well as community group and team activities offered by agencies and municipalities. Schools often accept practicum students who can assist in inclusive physical education classes and in before- and after-school programs. Similarly, hospitals also accept practicum students who can work as assistants in programs that introduce physical activity for patient recovery. In industry, private fitness centers frequently encourage the participation of practicum students to improve their services to clients with disabilities. And, finally, many special programs such as Goal Ball, Special Olympics, and Paralympics have been designed for people with disabilities. Most of these programs welcome practicum students. Table 1.1 offers a lengthy, though not exhaustive, list of possible placements for practica.

Practicum Processes

To fulfill APA practicum requirements, your placement will be in a program that includes or services people with disabilities, or you might work in a one-on-one relationship with one person who has a disability. Approval of placements depends on how well the APA course objectives for practica can be achieved in the placement you choose.

Practica are completed in conjunction with the APA course. The duration of the practicum depends on the requirements established by the instructor of your APA course—generally between 10 and 15 weeks during the academic term in which the APA course is offered. Although you might have a specific number of hours required of you for APA requirements, if you're committing to a program, you might need to

Table 1.1

Potential Practicum Placements

Type	Possible locations	Examples of skills and knowledge that would be an asset	In addition to getting to know some great people, you might learn about . . .
Physical education classes	**SCHOOLS**		
	Inclusive programs and programs in schools for children with specific disabilities		
	Public		
	Kindergarten	Like working with children	Managing groups of children
	Elementary	Elementary and developmental games	Introducing activities using lead-up games
	Middle schools	Sports	Adapting sports for inclusive participation
	High schools	Fitness activities	Adapting fitness equipment for all
		Lesson planning	Curriculum development
	Private		
	Preschools	Modifying activities and equipment	Accountability to the boards
	Kindergarten	Willingness to adopt the school culture	Assessing performance
	Elementary	Communication	Communicating with parents
	Middle schools	Planning	Flexibility
	High schools	Safety	
Recreational activities	**COMMUNITY CENTERS**		
Sports		Sports rules	Adapted bowling
Exercise classes	Gym	Exercise physiology	Tai chi, yoga
Swim programs	Swimming pools (aquatic centers)	Swimming	Aqua exercising
Fitness classes	Weight room	Exercise prescription	Circuit training
	Workout room	Treadmills	Spin classes

Exercise therapy	INSTITUTIONS		
Exercise classes	Hospitals		Physiotherapy
Rehabilitation	Extended-care facilities		Occupational therapy
			Recreational therapy
	Universities	Collecting data	Research
	CLINICS		
	Cardiac rehabilitation	Exercise physiology	Monitoring exertion
	Multiple sclerosis clinic		Exercise prescription
			Safety issues
Privately run programs	PRIVATE CLUBS		
	Country clubs, office towers	Fitness and sport development	Business of fitness and sports
		Interpersonal skills	
	CAMPS		
	Wilderness camp	Hiking, climbing, orienteering	Group dynamics
	Summer camp		Patience
	School camp		
	FAITH-BASED		
	Church, synagogue, mosque, or affiliated property	Interest and respect	Spirituality
Segregated programs			
Disability-specific programs, such as a weekly evening program for children who are deaf	University (on-site) programs	Teaching, coaching	
		Instructional signing	Pedagogy
			Research
Daily programs for children with severe intellectual disabilities	Schools		Programming
Specific for people with disabilities	COMMUNITY		
Therapeutic riding	Stables	Horseback riding	Adaptive devices for mounting horses
	Riding arenas		Cerebral palsy
Electric wheelchair hockey	Community hall	Stick-handling	Wheelchair maneuverability

(continued)

Table 1.1 *(continued)*

Type	Possible locations	Examples of skills and knowledge that would be an asset	In addition to getting to know some great people, you might learn about . . .
Therapeutic climbing	Recreation centers	Wall or mountain climbing	Building trust
Special Olympics	Ice rinks, swimming pools, track and field, gyms, soccer field, etc.	Coaching	Floor hockey
		Scoring	Bowling
Paralympic training	Swimming pools, gyms, track and field, etc.	Timekeeping	Paralympic slalom
Wheelchair sports	Community gyms	Basketball, tennis, etc.	Wheelchair basketball
Camps			
	Wilderness camps	Instructor	Sign language
	Residential	Don't get homesick	Wheelchair slalom races
Group homes			
Recreational	Residential areas	Home keeping skills	Board games
Shelters			
	Sheltered workshops	Workplace fitness	Exercising in a work environment

complete more hours than are required. Table 1.2 provides an example of the steps you will follow in getting your practicum started.

Earlier we identified several settings in which practicum placements commonly occur. Keep in mind that depending on your choice of setting, you might extend the hours of personal time required for completion of your practicum. For example, if you choose a community program many miles from your home or school, you might spend extra hours each week commuting to the practicum; these hours do not count toward the practicum. Your practicum hours are logged according to actual participation in the program.

In addition to a placement in one program, practica are also completed through attending programs at various locations. This type of practicum exposes you to different programs for people with disability. For example, one week you might be at a wheelchair basketball practice, the next week in a school physical education program, and the following week at a rehabilitation aquatics program. Alternatively, your practicum could be set up at your university, or you might be participating in a predesigned program that relies on practicum students to ensure its ongoing delivery. Learning about professional practice is exciting and insightful. Remember that you're in the practicum to learn. You bring special gifts and talents to your placement that

Table 1.2

Getting Started

What	Why	How
STEP 1		
Course requirements. These will be outlined in your course syllabus (or your instructor will clarify them for you).	Successful practica can look very different, depending on your college or university program and on location. If your instructor has pre-planned your practicum, there's no point in continuing further with this table—good luck in your practicum.	Practicum requirements vary; for example, here are four different placement requirements: 1. 10 weeks with a minimum of 1 hour per week, or 2. 20 hours required, but duration varies 3. 3 hours per week for 12 weeks, or 4. Time irrelevant. You must participate in a weekend event. You will help plan, organize, and run the event. Or, you will take the time needed to participate in four events chosen from a list of six provided by your course instructor.
STEP 2		
Choose placement	This is an opportunity to practice what you're learning in your APA course. You'll learn about yourself and meet new people.	Your instructor might have already chosen it for you. If not, complete the exercises at the end of chapter 1. These will help you select the best placement for you. If your instructor provided options, refer to those; if not, check table 1.1 for ideas on finding an appropriate placement.
STEP 3		
Making a contact	It's important that you make contact with the organizer of the program in which you would like to be placed. They might have questions that you're best equipped to answer. Another reminder: Complete exercises 1.4 and 1.5 at the end of this chapter before you contact anyone.	Your instructor might have provided a contact list. If not, you might be searching in the phone book or on the Web for information about the program of your choice. In this case, check with your instructor to make sure that your choices are appropriate.

will help you succeed in your work, and it's important for you to use these skills while never losing sight of the purpose of the practicum—to help you learn and grow as a professional.

Service delivery in APA is a dynamic and changing concept. To understand the complexities and issues, you're participating in real-life situations. You're given the additional opportunity to contemplate your personal and professional philosophy, question your practices, and consider new possibilities for the future.

A Practicum Is and Is Not

Although your experiences might be similar to those of a volunteer, your responsibilities significantly differ. You'll be participating in the practicum with a specific agenda related to the new skills and knowledge that you're acquiring in your APA course. You'll be documenting learning exercises in your manual (workbook) that relate directly to your practicum, and you'll be recording your personal learning journey in your journal (see appendix). You're encouraged to examine the models and theory of service delivery in APA in relation to your practicum experience.

Phases of a Practicum Placement

Your practicum is a personal journey. Like any good journey, it starts with preplanning. You have to determine your route, what you'll need to follow that route, and what you would like to do at various points along the way. At the end of your travels, you'll have images and stories that chronicle your adventure. Enjoy the journey!

Prepracticum

If you're selecting a practicum from several options, first make a list of the experiences you have that might relate to your practicum experience (see exercise 1.4 at the end of this chapter). Next, identify your goals and preferences in terms of the type of placement for your practicum. You might have the option to choose, or your instructor might have prearranged your placement. If you're choosing your placement yourself, questions to consider include the following:

- What experience will be most useful in helping your career possibilities?
- What are the types of possible learning opportunities?
- What's the proximity of the setting to your home or school?
- How well does the type of program align with your preferences?
- How does the practicum fit into your schedule?

TIP Megan's only part-time job has been at a large supermarket chain. She doesn't think that it relates to practicum. "When would scanning, cashing, and bagging have anything to do with my practicum?" Those are valuable tasks for her job, but it's the skills she has developed during the execution of these tasks that are important. For example, Megan has developed her interpersonal skills. She has patience and understanding in awkward situations. Customers frequently complain to her about food costs. She has developed initiative. She finds ways to be productive when her checkout lane isn't busy. She's learned to be flexible in the workplace. She doesn't always work the cash register; she is frequently asked to cover the customer service desk and occasionally the in-store flower shop. All of these skills are transferable to other situations where she might work with people.

When you've completed exercise 1.4 you'll have created a profile of your experience that includes your previous work experience, volunteer experience, course work, special skills or hobbies, and your personal preferences for a placement.

Initiating the Practicum

Your first step might include contacting a specific person, someone generally in conjunction with a program, agency, or institution, or making an inquiry through e-mail or a Web site. Deciding whom to contact depends on the setting and type of program at your placement. For example, if the program you're interested in relates to swimming instruction, you would need to figure out if the swimming instructor, the program coordinator for swimming, or the agency program director is the best person to communicate with.

Once your placement is finalized, learn as much as you can about the agency, school, or organization that's hosting the practicum. Give particular attention to the policies, goals, and objectives as determined by those providing the program. The best way to do this is to go to the Web site or to call and ask for brochures and other relevant information.

In some cases, your APA instructor might arrange everything for you. In other situations, your instructor might provide a list of contact names, or those contacts might be found in volunteer recruitment literature. Alternatively, you might have to phone an agency, school, or the general telephone number at the institution. For instance, say you want to work with someone who's visually impaired. You could start with a phone call to the local institute for people who are blind and ask about the existence or availability of sports and recreation programs. Turn to exercise 1.5 at the end of this chapter to be guided through an appropriate conversation.

Enjoying Your Practicum

Remind yourself of your personal expectations for the practicum. Create a learning plan; ask questions, lots of questions, of those who can help you. Talk to your supervisor, your instructor, and fellow workers, and most important, establish a relationship with the people with whom you work. This is your opportunity for first-hand experience with service delivery in APA. In chapter 2 we review the preliminary information to help you get started in your practicum; we also introduce the idea of asking critical questions. In this initial phase, focus on questions about what your responsibilities will be, what you're expected to do, whom you'll be reporting to, how to sign in or sign out, and so on. You'll feel good about the contribution you're making if you know what's expected of you and you're able to work toward those expectations. Don't be afraid to ask.

Practicum Review

A review of your practicum experience encompasses several perspectives. First, you'll evaluate your own performance; then participants might be asked for feedback; after that, the overall program might be reviewed. Evaluating the quality of your work is the responsibility of you, your supervisor, and your instructor. At the conclusion of your practicum you'll evaluate how well personal expectations, goals, and objectives have been met. But before you reach that point, you should do an interim evaluation. At about halfway through your practicum, complete a self-evaluation and request an evaluation from your supervisor. You'll learn how to evaluate yourself and review your achievements in chapter 8. Try to be realistic and refer to your journal for evidence of your progress. Then look at areas that can be improved. Perhaps you need to spend time preparing or maybe you want to develop your listening skills. An interim evaluation at this stage in the practicum is called a formative evaluation because it can assist you to grow and improve in the ways that you contribute to the practicum program. A review midway through the practicum lets you know how you're doing before it's too late to change things, if necessary, before the experience is over. This evaluation is also a chance to identify areas of the program that should be changed.

You might have the opportunity to give feedback to the host of the program. Program evaluation is often left to the participants, but hosts can receive valuable information about the success of a program from staff, volunteers, and practicum students.

The exercises at the conclusion of chapter 9 help you review and understand the types of information that can be most helpful to an organization.

Leaving the Practicum

Remember that the most important part of enjoying your practicum is establishing a relationship with the people you work with. They'll want to know in advance when you'll be leaving. Give them the exact date that you'll end your practicum so that there are no surprises. This allows you an opportunity to discuss the time that you have spent together and say good-bye. Take as much care in your departure from the practicum as you did in the prepracticum preparation.

Changes to Service Delivery

Ability is a contextual variable that's dynamic over time and circumstances (Fletcher, 2002). When ability is the focus, there's no separation among people who are categorized as disabled and those who are not. An ability or skill is part of a continuum of

By focusing on the ability, you create an atmosphere where there's no separation among people who are categorized as disabled and those who are not.

function. Recent changes in service delivery APA have seen perspectives in functional ability shift from what a person can't do to what he or she *can* do.

Abilities-Based Approach

Emes, Longmuir, and Downs (2002) introduced an abilities-based approach to service delivery defined by its emphasis on an environment designed to support the participation of individuals of all abilities. The focus is on the whole person in a learning environment, not the disability and not the activity. This approach is a philosophy toward service delivery, not a model for service delivery.

The basic tenet of an abilities-based approach is that each person has a unique constellation of functional abilities on which service delivery should be focused. The abilities-based approach compares the functional abilities of a person with the demands of activities and measures the extent of compatibility between the two. Factors that influence the success of an abilities-based approach include the principles of person-centeredness, inherent inclusiveness, individualization, and environmental compatibility.

Person-Centeredness

The principle of person-centeredness places the person for whom an activity or program is being planned at the center of the planning process (O'Brien & O'Brien, 1998). Person-centeredness suggests that the professional move from a superior role of expert to the more humble role of a partner interested in supporting individual interests, participation, and learning needs. Thus, attention in an abilities-based approach is directed away from asking, "What's different about this client, and how can I change him or her to better 'fit' with everyone else?" and toward questions such as, "What are your personal interests, capacities, and abilities? What supports do you need to express them?" (O'Brien & O'Brien, 1998, p. 20). Person-centered planning does not ignore disability—it simply shifts the emphasis to a search for capacity in the person.

> Raynor is in the 7th grade. He has muscular dystrophy and uses a wheelchair. Thinking about Raynor's capacity, Leanne entered the following into her journal: "I brought *Bop-It*, a hand coordination game, with me to our first time together. R is very ambidextrous, even though his arms are somewhat rigid. *Bop-It* is a game that asks a player to "bop it," "pull it," or "twist it." Playing the game increases reaction time and arm–hand movement. This was also a good way to break the ice and show R that we could have fun together. We played for a bit, passing back and forth on the same team; then we set level goals, and R tried to get there. As the game progressed, R's reaction time decreased, and the speed of his arm and hand movements increased as well. R seemed to enjoy this and opened up a bit while playing."

Inherent Inclusiveness

In an abilities-based approach to APA, inclusion is not considered an event or a method in which all students with disabilities are educated with their nondisabled peers in regular classes. Rather, inclusion is a value that's inherent in good service delivery. Inclusion is a social imperative that promotes the creation of communities that support all of their members and ensures they share equitably in its resources regardless of their differences (Jeffreys & Gall, 1996).

Inclusion is often mistakenly used interchangeably with the word "integration," but there's a significant distinction between the two terms. *Integration* is defined as adding something to an existing whole and usually addresses efforts to manage the reversal or reduction of segregation. Integration doesn't necessarily result in inclusion because proximity doesn't guarantee acceptance. *Inclusion,* ensuring that all parts must be included to create the whole, can't occur without attitudes of acceptance and a commitment to respect the rights of and value all members of society equally.

It has become evident over time that inclusion (physically, socially, and emotionally) is the outcome of valuing people regardless of their differences. The abilities-based approach begins with creating an environment that serves everyone. Thus, in physical activity, inclusion means that all interested individuals have equal access to full participation with peers at all times.

Individualization

An abilities-based approach clearly shifts the emphasis from remediating deficits to maximizing abilities. LaMaster, Kinchin, and Siedentop (1999) reported that specialists who teach elementary physical education found that the more inclusive the class, the more individualized the planning and delivery had to be. Individualization suggests planning and program delivery based on abilities and, as a result, learning and successful participation is enhanced for *every* participant, with or without disabilities.

Environmental Compatibility

The ultimate key to an abilities-based approach is the compatibility of the environment in which services are delivered. In the past, negative and stereotyped attitudes have restricted the full involvement of people with disabilities in regular sport and recreation programs. The attitudes and behaviors of generic service providers are critical, and the physical, social, and psychological accessibility of the places in which they practice is fundamental to an accepting environment.

Focusing on You and Your Learning Experience

Learning while engaged in practice activities (practicum) is part of a model of learning that's well described by Kolb (1984). He identifies a model of *experiential learning* that begins with a concrete experience (an experience in your practicum), followed by a phase of reflective thinking and observations (your journaling and talking with others). The experience becomes meaningful during the next phase, when those reflective thoughts and observations are assessed in relation to theory you've studied (the classroom part of your APA course), and this new learning can be tested in different situations (your next practicum experience). Kolb's model is depicted as a recurring cycle within which the learner tests new learning through ongoing reflection and conceptualization (figure 1.1).

Before engaging in the concrete experience of your practicum, it's important to learn more about yourself. A good understanding of your personal values and attitudes along with an assessment of the skills that you bring to the practicum will help you reflect on and conceptualize meaning during your experiences.

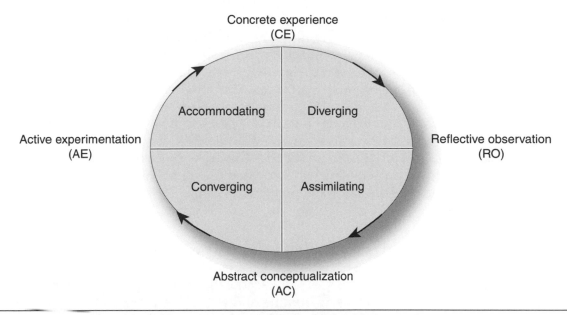

Concrete experience
(CE)

Active experimentation
(AE)

Reflective observation
(RO)

Abstract conceptualization
(AC)

Accommodating

Diverging

Converging

Assimilating

Figure 1.1   The experiential learning cycle and basic learning styles (Kolb, 1984).

KOLB, DAVID A., EXPERIENTIAL LEARNING: EXPERIENCE AS THE SOURCE OF LEARNING AND DEVELOPMENT, 1st Edition, © 1984. Reprinted by permission of Pearson Education, Inc., Upper Saddle River, NJ.

Self-Awareness: Understanding Your Values, Attitudes, Expertise, and Ethics

As you've likely heard, actions speak louder than words. We reveal our true selves through the way we behave. Our behavior is guided by our values, attitudes, expertise, and ethics. We can learn about ourselves by developing our self-awareness.

Values

Participating in the practicum should allow you to consider the values you hold and how they influence you in your practice. Values are fundamental understandings that influence how you think, your perspective or view of things, and the decisions you make. We choose our values freely, and they always represent a choice among alternatives. Values are persistent in our lives and significantly influence our behavior. Talking about something doesn't necessarily reflect our values; it's in the actions we take that our values are evident. For some of you, this might be the first time you've clarified your values for yourself. Exercise 1.1 at the end of the chapter gives you the opportunity to consider your values in association with service delivery in adapted physical activity.

Attitudes

Your mental attitude affects the way you live your life. It influences your way of thinking, how you feel, your emotions, and your opinions. Attitude significantly affects the experience you'll have in your practicum. Consider the variables you might encounter in your practicum that affect your feelings, opinions, and perhaps emotions. These variables might include people at the practicum site (supervisors, co-workers, program participants), the types of activities provided for the participants, methods used to deliver the program, and the program venue or environment. Everyone involved will likely view the situation in a slightly different way. For example, in previous situations, such as playing on an interscholastic team, you probably heard others speak about the circumstances of the team in different ways. Their perspective might have been more positive or more negative than yours. They might have had concerns about things you hadn't even considered. Regardless of what people respond to in this type of situation, their words and behavior reveal their attitude. Ask yourself, What are the factors that characterize positive and negative attitudes? Exercise 1.2 at the end of this chapter asks you to identify factors that you associate with a positive attitude, how you perceive your own attitude, the ways you demonstrate that attitude, and how a positive or negative attitude affects the practicum setting.

Expertise

Many students in physical education and kinesiology programs are athletes, fitness advocates, or volunteer coaches of community teams. Previous work experience often includes working at summer camps, holding leadership positions at recreational centers, or instructing sports such as swimming and skating. These types of activities, along with the education you're receiving in your degree program, contribute to the lifelong exercise of building your professional expertise. In your practicum placement, you might be viewed as an expert because of the nature of your experience and the material you're studying in your major. At the end of the chapter (exercise 1.4) you're asked to do a self-assessment of your unique abilities and experiences and explain how they contribute to your evolving expertise.

Ethics

During the course of your practicum experience, you'll be working with a person or persons who have disability. Your work will take place in an activity environment that might include other practicum students, volunteers, and professionals such as fitness leaders, teachers, exercise therapists, physiotherapists, nurses, and other service providers. Wherever and whenever we interact with other humans and provide service, we're faced with making decisions that affect the lives of those we're interacting with. This holds true in your practicum as well. Understanding the importance of human relationships is the key to good service delivery. Building strong, positive relationships with people is most easily achieved when you're practicing the highest level of ethical behavior. As a future professional, you have a responsibility to consider the ethical implications of your choices and your personal behavior.

Ethical decisions and behavior are good, fair, decent, moral, and principled. The following are examples of the principles that guide the delivery of service in adapted physical activity.

• **Competence.** As a practicum student you're expected to demonstrate a level of competence that reflects both the program of study that you've completed to date plus the previous experience you've acquired through work and volunteering. You should provide services and represent yourself as competent within the boundaries of your education, experience, and any credentials you have acquired, such as certification in fitness training.

• **Sensitivity.** No one likes having their weaknesses exposed or beliefs berated. We generally don't like to be embarrassed. Acting as caring human beings can help us avoid uncomfortable situations. In adapted physical activity you should be highly sensitive to someone with a disability because his or her concerns might be unique and in some cases unexpected. For example, a learner might not want to be removed from his or her wheelchair. Another might have difficulty speaking clearly, but he or she is not deaf and is extra sensitive to people raising their voices around her.

• **Facilitate learning.** Your main responsibility is to facilitate learning and participation in an activity. In the process, you should encourage autonomy, independence, and self-determination in the participants. Failure to do this usually occurs if you come to your placement unprepared or if you encourage the person you're working with to do things that are more satisfying for you than for him. It can be gratifying to do things for other people because it makes us feel useful and helpful. This approach can lead to more dependence rather than independence. Always ask yourself if you are promoting independence. According to your knowledge, it's also your responsibility to ensure that this person is made aware of other activity opportunities that exist in the community. In general, when you keep the best interests of your learners foremost in you mind, you're likely to be facilitating their development.

• **Confidentiality.** In adapted physical activity, the relationship between the practicum student and the participant is based on the right to privacy and confidentiality. For instance, you might have access to a learner's health reports, performance

Encourage autonomy, independence, and self-determination in the participants as you facilitate learning and participation in activities.

assessments, participation notes, and so on, but none of the information in these or similar documents should be disclosed without the express written consent of the participant or her parents or guardian. Your conversations should always be considered confidential. You should not repeat anything you've heard from participants if doing so breaches their privacy.

- **Respect.** Your interactions with people participating in adapted physical activities should be based on mutual respect. Respect the inherent dignity and worth of all people. You show your respect for participants by using people-first language and listening actively to what they have to say. Respect is further reflected in your attempts to enhance the capacity of those you're working with. Supporting advocacy initiatives is another example of demonstrating respect. Also respect the other service providers with whom you're working. Recognize their opinion and acknowledge their competence. Avoid conflicts, particularly in front of participants. Never make derogatory comments about a peer. Use professional language and cooperate with peers and colleagues.

Summary

"Practice, then, determines the development and progress of knowledge, and theory and practice are interdependent." (Vazquez, 1977, p. 172)

Practicum is experiential learning. It refers to the part of the program that engages you as a learner in active practical learning within and beyond the normal instructional setting. Your work in practica can lead to broader, more enduring learning outcomes (Kolb, 1984). The relevance of the experience can be assessed and placed into context through reflective observation. The most exciting thing about this kind of learning is that it's open-ended in the sense that neither you nor your instructor has prior knowledge of all the results. This chapter should have you prepared to begin this exciting form of learning.

Exercise 1.1
Values Confirmation, Self-Awareness, and Ethics

Complete the following sentences

1. When I meet a person for the first time, the thing I notice first is . . .

_____

2. A person who uses a wheelchair . . .

_____

3. If I received a severe spinal cord injury in an accident, I would . . .

_____

Tell your story

You and a classmate (someone you don't know well) inform each other about someone you're an expert on—yourself. For 3 to 5 minutes you'll talk about yourself while your partner takes notes. While you tell the story, your partner will record key words (actual words used by the storyteller). Key words are those used by the storyteller to describe things, qualities, activities, values, and ideas that are important to this person. They might reveal recurrent themes or describe an ethical stance, or they might just describe things the storyteller feels very strongly about.

4. In the space provided in the table, write down the phrases or key words that your partner recorded while you were speaking. Next, write down the values that you believe to be important to you. These two lists might coincide or might not. How well they match can help you learn more about yourself.

This section is for the key words your partner recorded:	This section is for you to record the values that are important to you:

5. In your estimation, how well do the two columns match?

_____

_____

Actions speak louder than words

6. It's time to consider whether you practice the values that you say are important to you. Begin by completing the following story.

Once I started to cross a very wide intersection, and just as I stepped off the curb the walk signal turned to stop. I decided to go for it and started to run. When I was halfway across the street, I overtook an elderly man walking slowly with a cane. It was clear the traffic lights would change long before he reached the other side. Not knowing what else to do, I . . .

_____

_____

_____

_____

_____

_____

7. Write down your own example of a time when your actions were obviously based on your values.

_____

_____

_____

_____

_____

_____

_____

_____

Exercise 1.2
Positive and Negative Attitudes

1. What is a positive mental attitude?

_____

_____

_____

2. Do you believe you have a positive or negative attitude?

_____

_____

3. In what ways do you demonstrate your attitude? List three examples of when and how your attitude was expressed through your actions.

_____

_____

_____

_____

4. What contributions does a positive attitude bring to the practicum setting? How does a negative attitude affect the same environment?

_____

_____

_____

_____

Words Are Important

"Person-first language" and "words with dignity" describe a way of speaking and writing that reflects a sensitivity and respect for other human beings. It's the type of language we should adopt regardless of whom we're describing or whom we're talking to, but often we speak of or to people with disability without realizing we're not using people-first language and words with dignity. The following exercises encourage you to think about the words you use and give you practice using appropriate language.

The Coalition for Active Living (2002) offers the following reminders:

- Describe the person, not the disability.
- Refer to a person's disability only when it's relevant.
- Avoid images designed to evoke pity or guilt.

The coalition offers the following examples:

Instead of . . .	Use . . .
Disabled, handicapped, crippled	Person with disability
Afflicted with, suffering from, victim of	Person with *or* person who has
Confined, bound, restricted to, or dependent on a wheelchair	Person who uses a wheelchair

Next to the following words, write descriptors that are more appropriate.

Instead of . . .	Use . . .
Retard, retarded	
Spastic	
Mental, mentally ill	

Prepracticum Preparation: Self-Assessment of Expertise

1. Write down all the work experience you have had in any job in which you were paid.

_____

_____

_____

2. Write down the skills that you acquired as a result of performing those jobs.

_____

_____

_____

_____

_____

3. List previous volunteer experiences you have had.

Name of program	Setting	Participants	Duration
1.			
2.			
3.			

4. List your courses and training or special skills that might be relevant to the practicum. Include your hobbies, participation in competitive sports (as an athlete, coach, trainer, or other capacity), and recreational activities (as a participant, leader, organizer, or other capacity) that have been part of your life. What skills have you developed as a consequence of participating in these activities?

_____

_____

_____

_____

TIP You may have learned many skills that you think might not be related to your practicum, but many might be useful skills that you'll end up using. For example, here are some skills other students learned in summer and part-time jobs:

- How to delegate jobs and organize activities (from a student who helped organize a statewide summer games event)
- Leadership and interpersonal skills (from a student who was a camp instructor)
- How to work under stressful situations (from a student who is a wildland fire fighter during summer months)
- Customer service skills (from a student who works in retail sales part time)
- Initiative and communication skills (from a student who is an assistant team manager)

5. If you're able to choose or have options for your practicum placement, list your preferences for practicum placements.

_____

_____

_____

6. Consider your existing time commitments and establish a realistic list of possible times for your practicum.

Day	Time	Exceptions

Initiating the Practicum: How to Get Started if Your Practicum Has Not Been Prearranged

Make notes using the following guide to get yourself going and to sound professional in your approach.

Begin with a contact (telephone, e-mail or Web site, name):

Phone:_____

E-mail or Web address: _____

Name of a contact person:_____

Introduce yourself and why you're calling:

Hello, my name is_____

and I'm calling because _____

_____ .

Review the requirements of the practicum:

- Offer to show your APA Guide, identify chapter 5, and describe how it discusses a supervisor's responsibilities and the expectations of the university or college.
- If your college has an affiliation agreement, offer to provide it to the organization. This type of agreement is usually a legal document or a formal statement of understanding that outlines the responsibilities of the educational institution versus those of the organization that hosts the placement (ask your instructor for assistance on this one).
- If appropriate, arrange a meeting.
- Confirm the starting time of the meeting, where it will occur, and the name of your supervisor.
- Ask about an orientation. Is one provided? At what times? Where?

If your practicum is prearranged:

- Confirm your placement with your course instructor or the agency or other setting in which you're going to practice.

- Ensure that you've completed any expectations for prepracticum preparation.
- Attend orientation, if appropriate.

Record the relevant information associated with your placement:

Your placement is _____

With program or agency _____

Where (facility) _____

Address (of facility) _____

Day(s) _____

Time(s) _____

Participant(s) _____

Your orientation will be on (date and time) _____

at (location) _____

Name of contact person or supervisor _____

Your starting date is _____

2

Learning Tools and Strategies

"A discovery is said to be an accident meeting a prepared mind."

Albert von Szent-Gyorgyi (1893–1986)

Chelsey talked about learning in her practicum in the following excerpt.

All in all, this was a great practicum, and I had a lot of fun and learned a lot. One of the biggest things I learned is although you can sit in a classroom and learn about how to do things, you really need to go out and put that knowledge to work. You need to get to know the participants and gear and focus the program around their needs, both individually and as a team (in this particular situation). I also met a bunch of really cool people and friends who took me in and treated me with respect and as one of the team. I hope to keep in touch with them and come back next year and be more involved with the team from the get-go and continue learning and growing alongside them.

Regardless of the specialization or career you choose—school physical educator, outdoor educator, exercise therapist, coach, physiotherapist, athletic therapist, occupational therapist, or a related field—your practicum will be meaningful experience in preparing you for the future. Each placement in which you work with people who have disability will offer new insights into how to improve your skills and techniques as a part of your journey toward becoming a professional.

You can use several tools to prepare yourself for a successful practicum experience. These tools help you learn more about yourself and guide your decision making in the context of your role in your practicum. They also lead you to think analytically about the events of your practicum, their meaning for you, and the cognitive and emotional impact they have on you.

In chapter 1 you completed exercises that focused on you. To begin with, understanding your personal values helped you to face some of the concerns you might have about undertaking a practicum, as well as your behavior and how you approach your responsibilities. Doing an inventory of your work, volunteer efforts, sport participation, and related activities allowed you to explore how your previous experience can help prepare you for your practicum. Examining your attitude toward service delivery for people with disability gave you a frame of reference for further understanding how to participate in your practicum. Now in chapter 2, we focus on learning tools and strategies you'll use during your placement.

Strategies for Successful Participation

You can do much to prepare yourself for your placement. First, find out in advance as much as you can about the location and agency (host) of the program. If you know who participates in the program, learn more about the participants. For example, if you're going to a swim program for people with multiple sclerosis (MS), find out what MS is and learn as much as you can about it. Look in a textbook, search on the Internet, or phone the MS society. Think about conversations you might have with participants in the program. Make a list of the things you might have to take with you to the practicum. This chapter outlines some of the key learning activities to help you succeed in your practicum.

Learn About Your Practicum Site

Your first opportunity to learn about the agency, school, or community program that is hosting your placement will probably be a scheduled orientation. If an orientation is not offered, then seek out relevant information either through written correspondence or a telephone conversation. Information most helpful in preparing to participate in a practicum includes the following:

- **A brief history and philosophy of the agency.** Learn about the purpose of the programs that the agency offers and the methods and procedures implemented within the organization.

- **Policy statements.** You need to understand the organization's position on such issues as dealing with disruptive participants, subsidizing fees for participants from low-income families, working in the volunteer program, and other issues.

- **Organizational structure.** Try to get clear on the relationships among the various personnel and programs in the agency or school and how they report to one another.

- **Programs.** The program placement for your practicum is probably only one of many programs offered by the institution or organization. Learning about other programs, classes, or courses allows you to pass information on to the participants with whom you work. There might be alternative opportunities available or advanced levels they might enjoy.

- **Environment and staff.** The work environment and the staff together create a culture within the organization that is an important aspect of the workplace. Learning about traditions and routines that have developed within your practicum setting will help you understand the methods of operation you'll encounter and the decision-making processes that occur.

Confirm your perceptions and understandings gleaned from the orientation you attended or the information you retrieved through conversations and written material.

Speak to your supervisor as issues arise; ensure that your understanding is indeed what is practiced at the program delivery level.

Roles and Responsibilities

In some cases you'll be given a description of practicum student responsibilities (often the same as volunteer responsibilities). This helps clarify the expectations about your performance and the procedures established in the agency. Keep in mind expectations are reciprocal (figure 2.1).

What you can expect from the agency:

- A person on staff (or a trained volunteer) who has been designated as your supervisor or contact person
- An orientation to the school, hospital, agency, or institution (in the form of a workshop, written materials, a meeting, or audiovisual presentation)
- Provision of agency expectations of you during your placement
- Feedback (either formal or informal) in the form of meetings, scheduled evaluations, or written feedback in your journal
- Review of your completed logbook
- Verification of your placement and activities as recorded in your logbook

Your role and responsibilities include the following:

- Know what's expected of you and work toward fulfilling those expectations. You are responsible to the host organization, your supervisor, participants, and *yourself.* If problems arise, don't bypass your supervisor unnecessarily. Contact your course instructor if you're having problems.
- If necessary, do background research on the specific disability, medical history, and other factors regarding the people with whom you're working.
- Ensure that your agency supervisor reads your completed journal.
- Obtain all signatures on the forms included in the placement manual.
- Review the final comments of your agency supervisor.

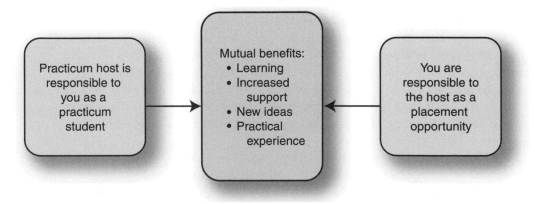

Figure 2.1 Mutual benefits and responsibilities.

Observing activities can help you determine the abilities of learners. You should know what your learners are capable of in order to help them reach their fullest potential.

Developing Good Observational Skills

The foundation of an abilities-based approach to adapted physical activity is to view participants as people with abilities and capacities for activity and learning. The process of engaging and involving learners to their fullest potential requires that you understand their abilities and build on them to facilitate successful participation. Identifying abilities and capacities is part of the planning process and begins with the process of observation.

When you observe activities in either a formal or informal setting, you are witnessing complex behaviors that are usually physical and verbal and tactile. You can observe activities that occur individually, with partners or in groups or teams, and within the context of a variety of environments, including gym, classroom, court, arena, field, pool, or wilderness trail. Observing can be fun and enjoyable, but learning how to record what you've observed can be challenging. Often when you observe you make assumptions about what you've seen based on your interpretation of what you're looking at. Have you ever talked to someone who looked and sounded very healthy only to learn later that he or she had been diagnosed with a serious illness? In fact, you saw her smiling and listened to her speaking with humorous comments and you interpreted that as good health.

It's difficult to focus only on what you see and not on what you think about the meaning of what you've seen. The first step in developing good observational skills is to practice looking at events, actions, behaviors, and settings and record *only* what you see, saying nothing about any corresponding judgments or evaluations you have made. At the end of this chapter you'll have an opportunity to practice writing good observational statements (exercise 2.1).

Establishing a Relationship With the Learners in Your Practicum

Getting to know the people you're working with in your practicum can be fun and might even be rewarding in the long run. You'll enjoy your interactions with the participants of your practicum more if you get to know them personally. Do keep in mind that this is a relationship that you're building for professional interaction, not for social engagement. Taking steps to get to know your students is intended to send a message that you're interested in them as individuals. They'll be interested in you, too. At the end of this chapter an exercise is provided that offers several suggestions on how to begin to establish a relationship with learners (exercise 2.2).

Learning From Your Practicum

When it comes to learning in your practicum, you're in the driver's seat. Take advantage of your time in the program to ask questions. Later, think about your experience and write about it in your journal. This process repeals itself through your practicum (figure 2.2).

Asking Critical Questions

To enquire is to seek learning by asking; critical to successful enquiry is posing good questions. If you ask good questions, you'll get valuable information. For you to provide the best service possible in APA, you'll want the best information available. Posing good questions also gives you the opportunity to challenge the status quo and to analyze information and make it meaningful and useful to planning and problem solving in APA. Don't ever get too comfortable with the way things have been done in the past— learning to be a professional includes seeking new solutions to old challenges.

Learning through enquiry is the basis of a pedagogical method called enquiry-based learning (EBL). It's the perfect vehicle to link the theory and knowledge you're studying in your course to real-life practice in APA. It also enhances your skills for lifelong professional development. Biley and Smith (1998) define this type of learning as "a method and philosophy of education that aims to develop analytical and critical thought, co-operative and self-directed learning and the integration of knowledge and

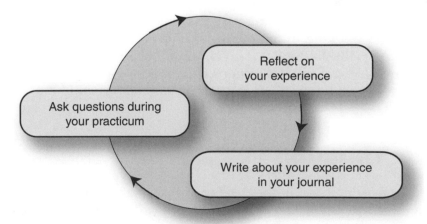

Figure 2.2 The repeating process of the practicum experience.

The instructor facilitates learning rather than controlling it using the enquiry-based learning (EBL) approach.

skills within the context of practice and self-motivation" (p. 1022). For the purposes of your APA practicum we'll focus on that aspect of EBL that deals with asking questions and analyzing information to learn more about a person or situation and to help solve problems. In EBL, fictional cases or scenarios that present realistic problems facilitate learning. In your practicum, the situations and scenarios are the real-life events and experiences that occur in your practicum. You'll use the same tools of learning, however, which are asking questions, gathering information, and formulating solutions to problems.

EBL uses an approach in which the course instructor's role is to facilitate learning rather than control learning. In a field in which knowledge and practice are constantly developing, it might be reasonable to accept that course teachers cannot be "founts of all wisdom." Nor is it desirable for them to be so, as such a prescriptive approach might tend to produce a dependent, rather than independent, learner.

Fundamental to working in a model that relies on abilities-based and person-centered planning is the concept of individualization. To provide service at an individual level, you must ask good questions to gain information about the needs and potential of a person. Exercise 2.3 at the end of this chapter will help develop your questioning skills.

Reflective Thinking

In chapter 1, Kolb's depiction of the cycle of experiential learning is described as an appropriate model to follow during your participation in a practicum. Recall that subsequent to the concrete experience, reflective thinking and conceptualization are outlined as the next step. When you think back on an experience, you begin the reflective thinking experience. Reflecting is a cognitive process that promotes self-assessment and self-awareness. To reflect on your experience, begin by asking yourself what you think about your personal contribution to the practicum. What do you perceive to be your strengths and weaknesses? Think about your feelings and compare them to how you have felt in the past during similar situations. Perhaps through reflective thinking you can develop a hypothesis about your work or the expected outcomes of your practicum experience. The most important aspect of reflective thinking is that it can generate new patterns of cognition. Question why things happen in the practicum in the way that they do. What patterns do you see emerging? What strategies can you use to change patterns that might have a negative impact on the outcomes of the practicum? Are there any unexpected patterns that you could capitalize on to improve practicum outcomes?

Take the time to focus on your understanding of meaning, values, and interrelationships that are unfolding for you through this experience. Your practicum is not just about delivering a physical activity program. You're also learning about human interaction and how verbal and nonverbal communication influence feelings, motivation, and responses. You have the opportunity to consider these factors in light of the social and political processes that are part of the environment in which you're practicing.

Journaling

The appendix contains space for you to make your personal journal entries. A journal is a personal record of participation in a practicum experience. Reflective journaling is a very personal learning exercise. Although collaboration and cooperative exercises are important factors in learning, journaling requires that you turn to yourself and reflect on your own personal experience. Journaling is an occasion for recording personal feelings, perspectives, and emotions. Your triumphs should be celebrated in writing; your challenges, failures, and disappointments should also be noted. Each contributes significantly to learning. Entries should reflect your personal journey, so they might differ in tone and content over the duration of your practicum. Review your journal entries from time to time and consider how your behaviors and reactions have changed. Look for themes or try to build a sense of development that might be reflected in your journal.

Journal entries might include information about events that occur during the practicum; observations about people, activities, and the facility or environment; and your reflections or response to these factors. The most significant part of the journal is your reactions to the events that have transpired during your practicum. Your interpretations are among the most dynamic and powerful aspects of your practicum. Thus, you should write in your journal in a timely fashion. The sooner you make an entry after a session, the more easily you'll remember important information.

One of the most effective ways to focus on learning during a practicum is to record what happened in each session. This is an opportunity to chronicle significant and meaningful events, but even more important is the process of writing. Writing about your practicum forces you to be reflective and critical of the experience; through this process you'll improve your learning.

Your logbook should include

- a record of facts, events, and process;
- a record of observations and experiences; and
- an appraisal of the personal impact of these events on you.

Journal writing can begin with an observation, a question, or a feeling, but the most important part of writing is to get started. The purpose of creating a journal is self-assessment; thus, the end product must be, among other things, meaningful to you. Some helpful guidelines for keeping a journal include the following:

- Develop a routine of writing in your journal immediately after (or close to) the time of your weekly practicum experience.
- Be brief, but get a point across.
- Use language that won't embarrass you when others read your journal.
- Balance entries by thinking in terms of opposites, such as strengths and weaknesses.
- Identify recurring patterns of interaction.
- Consider the language you use and the thinking that it reflects (see Bloom's taxonomy in chapter 6).
- Recognize changes in your behavior, thinking, and self-awareness.

The words "reflect" and "reflective" have been used in this section to describe an important process used in journal writing. Refer back to the section of reflective thinking. Reflective thinking is a way to begin the journaling process, but it's also a significant learning process—one in which you learn about yourself.

 The following questions will help you create *reflective* entries in your journal.

1. How did you feel when you first arrived at your practicum? Were you nervous? Were you surprised by the size of the group or the facility? What had you expected compared to what you first confronted? *Five weeks into your practicum compare your feelings with those of your first entry. Ask the same questions.*

2. How well are you communicating with others? Why did you qualify your communication in this way?

3. Are you contributing in a way that is satisfying to you? What's going well? Why?

4. What's most rewarding for you? Why is it so rewarding? How does it make you feel?

5. What are you most proud of when you're at your practicum? Is it something you do? Is it a relationship you've established? Is it what you feel you've accomplished? Why does it make you feel proud?

6. What's the biggest challenge you face? If you could change one thing about your practicum, what would it be? Why do you want to change it? What difference would it make?

7. Do you have the support you think you need for successfully participating in your practicum? How can you improve your practicum support? What resources are available for you to use? Which ones have you used? How did that work out?

8. What are the surprises? Do unexpected things happen? What impact does this have on you and others? How do you think they feel? How do you feel?

9. What are you learning? How do you know? How do you feel about this outcome?

10. How does participating in this practicum affect you in other parts of your life? Why do you think it has this effect?

Your journal also gives you the chance to identify the extent to which you have integrated your learning in courses that deal directly with APA, as well as those that support your understandings in APA. You might want to compare how things in the field are done differently—how reality might or might not reflect theory. Remember that this is a personal journey; learning during this journey and writing about the learning should not be the same for any two individuals. To help you get started, there's a checklist exercise (exercise 2.5) at the end of this chapter.

Summary

This chapter presents the process of your participation in a practicum placement. Each skill will be used and will develop over the course of your experience. The skills of establishing a professional relationship, observing and recording behavior, asking critical questions, thinking and writing reflectively, and journaling will be important to your engagement in the practicum learning process. Use them for each practicum session.

Exercise 2.1
Recording Observational Statements

To help you understand the difference between a good observational statement and a statement that reflects an interpretation on what was observed, refer to the examples in table 2.1. Note that a good observational statement focuses on the behavior or actions being observed. It doesn't include any conclusions or assumptions drawn from the expressed behavior. When you read statements that "need work," you'll notice that you immediately begin to wonder why that statement was made.

Table 2.1
Informal Observational Statements I

Needs work	Good statement
Good spatial awareness with respect to other students and environment.	Consistently self-propelled her wheelchair into open spaces during group work.
She performs motor skills well with her upper body.	She pulled herself up an incline board using her arms.
He has good social interaction skills and competent cognitive abilities.	He talked and laughed with two other boys in the class and followed the teacher's instruction to "change stations, now sit down and put your hands on your knees."

Now read the statements in table 2.2 that need work and try to imagine what action or behavior might have led to the conclusion or assumption expressed in the statement. In the space provided write an observational statement that reflects only the action or behavior that could have resulted in that type of statement.

Table 2.2

Informal Observational Statements II

Needs work	Better statement
Demonstrated competent motor skills; good awareness of balance and coordination.	
She was not limited to her wheelchair; she was challenged to move her body in different ways other than in a sitting position.	
She seems to have good cognitive function; she understood what was going on.	
Integrates well with others but seemed to have difficulty comprehending verbal instructions.	

Exercise 2.2

Establishing a Working Relationship With the Person at the Center of Your Practicum

In the process of establishing a working relationship, you'll interact with a participant(s) by sharing ideas, a joke, a personal story, or something that's unique to either or both of you. This type of exchange builds understanding and trust among people; when understanding and trust are present in a relationship, learning is more likely to be more effective. The following exercises offer ideas for getting to know someone on a personal level. Obviously, the types of questions you ask children differ from those you would ask a teen or an adult.

Suggestions

1. Ask questions about . . .
   - Family (Can you tell me about your family? Do you have brothers and sisters? Who are you closest to? Do you have any cousins who live in another country?)
   - Name (How do you spell your name? What's your nickname? Why do people call you that?)
   - Reasons for attending the program (Are you here to learn more about . . . ?)
   - Likes and dislikes (What's your pet peeve? What's your favorite book, movie, TV show?)
   - Goals and objectives (What do you want to accomplish? How will you do it?)

- Length of time in the program (How long do you want to pursue this program? How long have you been in it?)
- Favorite foods (What do you eat when you're feeling down?)
- Expectations for their life (What will you do when you grow up?)
- Current perceptions (How do you see yourself at this point in time?)
- Jobs (Do you have a job? What do you do? Do you like it? Why?)
- Favorite holidays (What did you do for the Fourth of July? How do you spend Thanksgiving?)
- Hobbies, spare time, favorite games (What do you do for fun?)

TIP   Ask the person you're working with what they would like to know about you. Confidential information is off limits.

2. Other activities
- Share a story about a personal object. Discuss something that holds a special meaning for the learner; then discuss something that holds a special meaning for you.
- Tell jokes.
- Smile.
- Have your student introduce you to a friend (someone who might be in the same class) or invite him or her to bring a friend, sibling, or parent to his or her session.

Exercise 2.3
Asking Critical Questions

Finish the following statements:

1. When I ask a friend, it's usually about . . . _____

2. When I ask a stranger, it's usually about . . . _____

3. When I ask about things (objects) . . . _____

Compare the questions you ask a friend to those you ask a stranger to learn more about each.

4. What are the differences? What type of question is most revealing? How do these questions compare to those that you ask about things (objects)?

_____

_____

_____

_____

_____

5. What words or phrases help make questions to others more meaningful?

_____

_____

_____

TIP   Think about when people ask you questions that are meaningful to you. How can you phrase questions that make them easier and more interesting for others to answer?

Exercise 2.4
Reflective Writing

What are the differences between statements of fact, statements of observation, and writing reflectively about an experience? Are there differences in the verbs you use to write sentences? Are there differences in the way you think about what you're going to write?

Think about the last time you ate out of the house, whether it was at a fast-food outlet, a sit-down restaurant, or a friend's or relative's house.

1. Write a statement of fact about the experience.

_____

_____

TIP   Remember, facts are information that is basically indisputable.

2. Write a statement of observation about your experience.

_____

_____

TIP   Observation statements describe what you saw, not what you think about what you saw.

3. Write a reflective statement about the experience.

_____

_____

TIP   Reflective statements record your understanding of meaning, your impressions, and your insights. For example, "Rob's balance while standing has improved to the point where he can stand with the use of a walker, supervised but unaided, for 30 seconds. Walking itself, though, hasn't really shown much improvement. I really don't think I've ever reflected on how complicated walking is before working with Rob. My ignorance led me to be a little optimistic in setting a time line for objectives."

Journaling

Turn to your personal journal at the back of this book. Select one of your journal entries and check off those points from the following list that are evident in your writing. In the space provided write out the example you have taken from that entry. Not every point is in every entry, but all points should be included across the entries you have created.

- What do (did) you want to focus on for this particular session (goal, objective [just in time], plan)?

Example: _____

- Facts, events, process

Example: _____

- Observations and experiences

Example: _____

- Impact on you: feelings

Example: _____

- Balanced entries—think of opposites (your strengths—things to build on versus areas that you'd like to improve)

Example: _____

- Discussion of your thoughts about your personal contribution to the practicum experience

Example: _____

- Your understanding of meaning, values, and interrelationships unfolding for you

Example: _____

- Identifying the extent to which you have integrated your learning with the undergraduate courses required for your degree program

Example: _____

- Comparing how things in the field are done differently and how reality might or might not reflect theory

Example: _____

3

Motivation

"A successful individual typically sets his next goal somewhat but not too much above his last achievement. In this way he steadily raises his level of aspiration."

Kurt Lewin (1890–1947)

For Elizabeth, the day ahead seemed filled with anxiety. She had never worked with anyone with a disability before. Quite honestly, she wouldn't have chosen to participate in this practicum, but it was required as part of her course. She couldn't imagine how this experience would relate to her life or her career goals. Plus, she knew nothing about working with someone who had "special needs." Her course instructor indicated that the kids with whom she would be working had some problems with obesity along with being generally awkward when it came to physical activities. Elizabeth could barely motivate herself to get ready for her practicum, so how in the world was she going to get these kids to join in the program?

In the scenario above, Elizabeth is struggling with issues related to motivation, both her own and that of the individuals with whom she'll be working. Elizabeth's instructor has provided her with external motivation; the practicum is a part of a course, and Elizabeth's participation will be rewarded with a grade that counts toward her course grade. External motivation is often provided by external reinforcement for the behavior of individuals. Examples of these external reinforcers include money, praise, desired objects, activities provided by others, and grades. The assumption on which external motivation and reinforcement is based is that people will "work" for desired rewards and initiate or change their behavior if the reward is desirable enough.

But what happens when the external reinforcement ends? Does the person continue to behave in the desired way? Sometimes. If as a result of learning the desired behavior the person is intrinsically reinforced by feelings such as success, competence, or gratification, the behavior itself becomes intrinsically motivating. Another possibility is that the person sees value in performing in the desired manner. For instance, Elizabeth might come to understand that the skills she's learning in her practicum would make her a better teacher regardless of the type of student with whom she works. Or she might realize that the professional behaviors she's developing during her practicum would help her future employment.

Intrinsic motivation can be reinforced by promoting feelings of success, competence, or gratification.

But let's say that the person does not associate the behavior with anything of value. Would the removal of the extrinsic rewards—money, a good grade, or praise—mean the behavior ceases or diminishes? That is certainly a possibility that the principles of behavior management attempt to consider.

Behavior Management

The control or modification of individual behavior focuses on principles of learning that use precise behavioral and instructional objectives and individual reinforcement strategies that are consistent. The first step is to clearly identify the behavior that is desired. In the case of Elizabeth and her practicum this could include her own behaviors and those of the participants in her practicum. Elizabeth's instructor might want Elizabeth to show up on time, attend every session, interact positively with participants, demonstrate knowledge and skills learned in the course, or accurately evaluate her own performance. Elizabeth might want her participants to take turns, attend every session, demonstrate skills in the physical activities, and treat her with respect. These behaviors then need to be stated in objectives that are measurable and observable and that state the criteria within which the behavior will occur. Next, the reinforcers must be identified. A primary reinforcer might be social praise, such as saying "good job" or giving a pat on the back; events or activities, such as going on trips, playing games, or watching TV; or tangible goods, such as food, toys, or other objects. Tokens are secondary reinforcers because they represent value that can be exchanged for primary reinforcers at a later time.

Obviously, the reinforcer you choose to use must be valued and desired by the people you're working with. For example, Elizabeth has decided to try using tokens to reward behaviors of her participants. She then needs to determine how many tokens it takes to create interest and how much value each token should have. Elizabeth is fortunate because the program where she's doing her practicum is sponsored by a local service club that has a toy drive every year, and she has access to some of the toys for the token program. The kids get to see the toys beforehand, and they understand that each toy has a token value that is possible for them to achieve. Because her group includes many children with obesity, she has avoided food as reinforcement. In a situation in which food would be an appropriate reinforcer, she would have to decide what type of food would best motivate certain behaviors—cookies, candy, peanut butter and jelly, ice cream, or fruit? Sometimes the decision is based on practicalities. For instance, ice cream might be less convenient because it needs to be frozen, whereas candy can usually fit into a small bag and be kept in a pocket.

Once her objectives have been developed and her reinforcers chosen, Elizabeth can develop her plan of implementation. For the plan to be effective, it must be fair—the reward must suit the behavior and be given immediately after participants exhibit the behavior.

Many other pieces need to come together to form a successful behavior management system. The shaping of behavior, frequency of reinforcement, revision of objectives, and use of extinction, negative reinforcement, and punishment are additional concepts you might want to explore.

Although many behavior management programs are developed by someone other than the learner, Elizabeth might also want to consider self-contracting—that is, making a plan for herself. For example, she might develop a behavior management plan that includes her goals and objectives for the practicum, choice of personal reinforcers, and schedule for reinforcement. She herself will implement and control all parts of the plan. Let's say one of the issues she's dealing with is getting her course reading completed before she attends her practicum each week. She knows if she does the reading, she'll feel better prepared for the practicum and will appear more competent. But those intrinsic rewards have not been enough to motivate her to get the job done. This being the case, she could establish reading objectives for herself that include the type of reading to be completed, the number of pages to complete, and the amount of time to read the pages. She could set a reward, such as an event—a hot bubble bath?—or tangible goods such as her favorite treat. She would deliver the reward to herself after accomplishing the behavior.

Systems Perspective of Motivation

Most people involved in your practicum are social beings. Bronfenbrenner (1979) suggests that learning and development occur as individuals interact in a reciprocal nature with others who are important to them. Through modeling, we learn about behaviors that are acceptable in our society. By observing others, we develop increasingly complex behaviors and patterns of behavior that are acknowledged by those in our social systems whom we personally value. For Elizabeth and those with whom she'll be working, it's important that role models learn to transfer power to the developing person. For this to happen, the role model must first acknowledge that the developing person is capable of assuming the power. Elizabeth's practicum supervisor is someone she respects, and she knows that her supervisor graduated from the university Elizabeth attends. They are close to the same age—just 6 years apart. As a role model, Elizabeth's supervisor is aware that he must demonstrate the skills and behaviors he expects from Elizabeth. As she develops, he will allow her to assume increasing responsibility for initiating skills and behaviors and for providing feedback about her success.

How does this acknowledgment occur? First, a person-centered philosophy is necessary. Language is an important factor, and "person-first" language is the first step. A second part of acknowledgment is developing a reciprocal relationship and pattern of communication with the developing person. Asking him or her what is important, clarifying goals, and valuing his or her responses are examples of reciprocity.

Blom, Lininger, and Charlesworth (1987) suggest that disability is a result of a mismatch between the environment and the person. In addition to the social environment discussed above, behavior occurs within a physical environment that facilitates or hinders certain types of behavior. People with problems related to attention might find a complex physical environment distracting, leading to difficulty in motivation. Physical environments might contain barriers for people with mobility problems. For someone using a wheelchair, sets of stairs can limit access and diminish motivation. Persons with limited vision might find that lighting and color contrast facilitate participation and consequently enhance motivation.

Mediating the environment becomes an important part of motivation. Mediation involves reconciling the discrepancies among the adequacy of the environment, the capacities of the person, and the requirements of the task. The ability of the individual in negotiating the complexities of the physical and social environments seems related to experience, expectations of self and others, stress and anxiety, and self-efficacy related to the tasks involved (Bandura, 1997). What could Elizabeth do to mediate the environment for herself? How could this affect her motivation?

Initially, she might identify the causes of her anxiety about the practicum. For example, in the social environment, does she feel that she lacks sufficient knowledge about the types of disabilities she might encounter? Does she have preconceived attitudes about people with disability? Regarding the physical environment, does she lack competence in the physical activities in which she'll be engaged? Is she unfamiliar with the physical environment of her practicum? After identifying the sources of her anxiety, she could develop a plan for dealing with them. The plan should include ways for Elizabeth to manage her "inner needs" for knowledge as well as possible methods of interaction within the physical and social environments of her practicum.

Elizabeth could use a similar strategy in tackling motivation issues among participants in her practicum. In this case, Elizabeth might assume the role of mediator and reconcile some of the discrepancies. She could also teach this role and the skills that accompany it to her participants. Recognizing the factors affecting the motivation and functioning of those with whom she'll be working might help her prepare for and feel better about her own experience.

Person-Centered Planning As Collaboration

Intrinsic motivation is typically referred to as an internal state that activates or energizes behavior. Franken (1994) adds the concepts of arousal, direction, and persistence to our understanding of motivation. Many researchers believe that different factors influence motivation to initiate a behavior compared to the factors related to persistence. For example, emotional or affective factors such as self-image or self-esteem appear to affect initiation, whereas volition or goal orientation affect persistence of behavior (Huitt, 2001). What's consistent in the literature on motivation is the importance of the individual in the motivational process. It's difficult to motivate a person to act if he or she is not energized to action.

Between 1979 and 1992, people interested in creating life experiences that are meaningful for people with disability searched for ways to systematically understand the personal goals of people with disability. The resulting process, person-centered planning, was introduced in chapter 1. The purpose of person-centered planning is learning through shared action that is collaborative in nature (O'Brien & O'Brien, 2000). The process is interactive and involves actively listening and reflecting with the person with the disability and those who care about him or her. Although many protocols are available for person-centered planning, they share the following beliefs (O'Brien & O'Brien, 2000):

- See the person before the diagnosis.
- Use ordinary language and images, not professional jargon.
- Search for the person's gifts and capacities.
- Strengthen the voice of the person and those who know him or her best.

This process of person-centered planning appears congruent with the literature on motivation. If we work together with someone to achieve his or her personal goals, then this work might be intrinsically motivating. What needs to happen for this collaboration to be effective? First, everyone needs to gather information, share information, and value the contributions of each person involved. This includes the individuals with disability with whom you're working in your practicum. Second, all involved must act with responsibility. Offering suggestions, taking assigned roles,

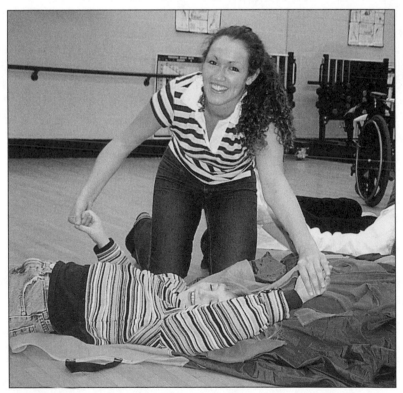

One of the beliefs of person-centered planning is to search for the person's gifts and capacities.

performing designated duties, and providing relevant information are examples of acting responsibly. Collaboration means valuing the viewpoints of others by listening to each person, allowing others to speak, taking turns in talking, and waiting to make decisions until you have considered everyone's viewpoints. Ultimately, the decisions in a person-centered planning process must be acceptable to the person with the disability.

What do you need to be truly collaborative when working with individuals with disability? John O'Brien (1997) suggests that true collaboration requires an understanding of the contrast between a difference model and an acceptance model.

Within the difference model, we see people with disability as

- different (not one of us),
- disconnected (not part of our communities or culture), and
- dependent (kept or managed).

Within the acceptance model, we see people with disability as

- individuals (like you and me),
- included (like you and me), and
- interdependent (like you and me).

Summary

External and intrinsic (internal) motivation are both factors in the behavior of individuals. External motivators are frequently objects, praise, activities, or symbols such as tokens that may be redeemed for rewards. Intrinsic motivation includes the personal reasons that exist within a person that cause him or her to behave in a certain way. For example, many of us do things because we feel good when we do them or when we are successful at doing them. We can use these concepts in developing programs that influence the behavior of the individuals with whom we work. However, it is imperative that we always focus on what the individual desires and frame the behavior program within that context.

The following chapter is devoted primarily to learning more about the collaborative process.

Exercise 3.1
Behavior Changes

1. Think about a behavior you want to change. Clearly identify the behavior in a sentence.

_____

_____

_____

2. Now, think about the types of reinforcers that are meaningful to you and list them.

_____

_____

3. For the next week, record the number of times you exhibit the behavior you want to change. It might help to keep a small notebook with you to ease your recording. List the time of day and what happened immediately before and immediately after the behavior.

_____

_____

_____

_____

_____

4. Analyze your data. What precedes the behavior? What are the conditions like when your behavior occurs? What is reinforcing the behavior (what happens after you behave in the way you have identified)?

_____

_____

_____

5. Now write a goal that specifies the change you want to make. Include such things as the degree to which you want to reduce the behavior (frequency), the date you want to have your goal accomplished, and any conditions you are imposing on yourself. Next, indicate how you will reward yourself if you are successful.

_____

_____

_____

_____

6. Now implement your behavior change plan. Make sure you record your feelings in your journal as you attempt to implement your plan.

4

Inclusive Teaming

"Disability is a matter of perception. If you can do just one thing well, you're needed by someone."

Martina Navratilova

A school system based on inclusive teaming through collaborative consultation requires a rethinking of typical service delivery systems (Andrews & Lupart, 1993, p. 241).

"Inclusive," "collaborative," and "consultative" are words now embedded in APA systems of delivery. We've moved away from cumbersome models of referral, assessment, and program placement that require hours of meeting time, extensive support staff, and vast financial and human resources. Inclusive schools and communities focus on immediate service delivery, planning, and problem solving.

Inclusive teaming is founded on the practice of collaborative consultation and the efficient allocation of school and community resources. Inclusive teaming is flexible, supportive, nonhierarchical, and designed to meet the needs of all children, learners, or program participants. How does this differ from traditional systems of delivery? Inclusive teaming relies not only on the instructor to monitor program success and participant satisfaction; input from parents, staff, other professionals, volunteers, and students is also part of the equation. Both formal and informal means are used to solve problems. Inclusive teaching is open and responds immediately to student needs, looking for commonsense, practical solutions.

Collaboration

The definition of collaboration suggests a process of working together and sharing for the mutual benefit of all parties. Stanovich (1996) identifies five criteria for successful collaboration:

1. Voluntary association
2. Parity among associates
3. Shared mutual goals
4. Shared resources
5. Shared accountability

Effective schools use their internal collaborative strength to reach out to the broader community. They mobilize their own resources and those of the community to build on their capacity for teaching and learning (Anderson, 1999, p. 29). Anderson also points out that collaboration is the cornerstone of developing a professional learning community in schools. Collaboration helps teachers focus on student work and change their teaching practices for better results. In this environment, roles and responsibilities can shift, and ultimately the school culture reflects new ways of thinking, working, and learning together.

Benefits of Collaboration

A primary benefit of collaboration is human interaction. The invigorating and social nature of collaboration is generally appealing to most professionals who work in human service. Collaboration is generally nonthreatening and supportive and is thus an attractive way to interact with people in schools and communities. Such interaction can occur in several ways. A standard interaction includes parents, students, teachers, and other professionals. Peer group interaction is a logical place to begin because each participant works within a setting that offers familiarities common to all. For example, students interacting with students share and understand the challenges of being "the learner."

Collaboration among professionals, such as teachers, has been successful in team teaching and shared teaching appointments. Parents' collaborating about shared resources and current information has been part of parent-driven agencies for children with disability for decades.

Inclusive teaming promotes collaboration across peer groups, such as between parents and professionals (teachers, occupational therapists, physiotherapists, speech and language clinicians, nurses, and doctors) or among teachers, parents, and students.

Lee (1999) points to the following advantages of working with a partner or a team:

- Intellectual stimulation for professionals
- Sharing of expertise
- Wide access to resources
- Benefit to learners from experiencing different teaching styles and perspectives

Collaboration provides rich opportunities for harvesting new ideas and developing established concepts. Preconceptions are more likely challenged within a collaborative system. By building on the expertise of others, collaboration enhances motivation and improves staff morale. Outcomes include teaching innovation, greater quality assurance, and connections to a wider sphere of expertise and resources.

Issues

Certain issues (Rich, Robinson, & Bednarz, 2000) can arise during the collaborative process, including loss of individual autonomy, which for many is the most threatening. In a multiskilled team, sharing is required, as Stanovich (1996) points out. For example, members share curricula, collaboratively produce resources, and agree on delivery. Sometimes it's difficult to let go of methods, techniques, and resources that have worked successfully in the past. Preparing curricula and developing lesson plans can be less efficient in a sharing collaborative arrangement.

Practicum students working as a team offers several benefits for both the practicum students and the learners.

The shift in roles and responsibilities and new relationships is associated with initial periods of uncertainty as teachers adjust to a new situation (Salend, Johansen, Mumper, Chase, Pike, & Dorney, 1997). Adjusting to something new or changing well-established routines and behaviors can be unsettling. There are so many things that might change, including daily prep time, how students are grouped, how they're monitored and evaluated, assignments, support available, and communicating with parents. Linert, Sherrill, and Myers (2001) identified the impact of level of commitment, personal concerns, organizational skills, and teaching philosophy on inclusive physical education classes. Teachers who were assigned to teach integrated classes were less committed than those who chose these classes. While some teachers express uncertainty and worry about the demands of including children with disability, others were excited about the challenge. High levels of self-confidence and perceived competence are important. Organizing classes with paraprofessionals that assist students with disability versus those classes without any assistance, unsatisfactory facilities (crowding) and equipment, and classes that are too short were all identified as requiring skill and commitment from the teacher. How teachers respond to or cope with concerns about the impact of including all students is influenced by their teaching philosophy. There can be a financial question related to the commitment that teachers make either directly or in-kind (researching information or attending workshops during their own time). These commitments can be challenging to track for accountability purposes.

Consultation

Another component of inclusive teaming is consultation. Inclusive teaching suggests that the APA specialist "serves as the 'expert,' providing suggestions that another teacher implements" (Lytle & Collier, 2002). The California Department of Education

(Lytle & Hutchinson, 2004, p.35) defines adapted physical education collaborative consultation as "a service that is provided on behalf of the student and assists the student in participating in the less restrictive setting of general and specially designed physical education." Three characteristic features define consultation (Block & Conaster, 1999). First, consultation is an indirect service because the consultant is not working directly with the student or person with a disability. Second, consultation is collaborative because the consultant works with others. Third, consultation is voluntary because the consultee requests the service from the consultant.

Depending on the request, a consultant can adopt various roles, such as advocate, researcher, trainer, educator, or facilitator. These roles require skills that are developed for use with various consumers, primarily other professionals such as teachers or instructors, parents and guardians, or children and adolescents. Regardless of the role, a consultant must have an expert knowledge level, good communication skills, and an ability to accurately and effectively document the consultative process. The exercise at the end of this chapter provides you with the opportunity to identify the potential team members that participate in inclusive teaming. As well, you will look at the process from both sides (i.e., consultant and consultee).

Summary

Inclusive teaming, based on collaborative consultation, ensures that the multiple professional responsibilities that are part of APA service delivery are shared among those who can best provide certain components of the service.

Exercise 4.1
Inclusive Team

1. In table 4.1, make a list of all the people who could be part of an inclusive team in APA. Beside each team member, describe the expert contributions he or she could make. If appropriate, complete this exercise using your practicum as an example. If not, consider all the "players" who are an important part of a person with disability being able to participate in a physical education class, a community fitness program, or a competitive wheelchair basketball league.

2. Consider the process of consultation and think about the skills essential for supporting positive interaction between a consultant and a consultee. In each column in table 4.2 list the most effective skills. In the consultant column, list the skills you would like to see in a consultant who is providing service to you. In the consultee column, do just the opposite—think of yourself as a consultant and list the skills that you would find most helpful in a consultee to whom you are providing service.

Table 4.1

Inclusive Teaming

Team member	Services
1.	
2.	

Table 4.2

Skills for Positive Interaction

Consultant	Consultee

(continued)

Table 4.2 *(continued)*

Consultant	Consultee

Part II

GETTING INTO IT:
Participation

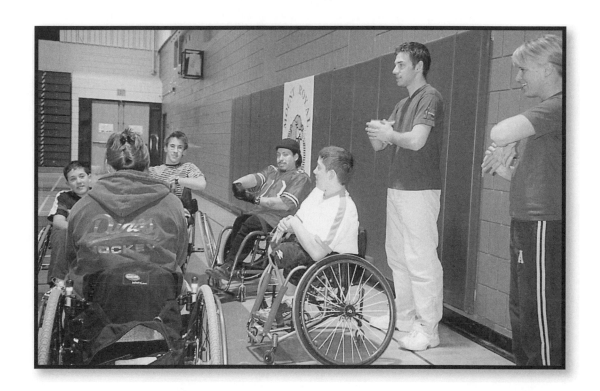

"You can know the name of a bird in all the languages of the world, but when you're finished, you'll know absolutely nothing whatever about the bird. . . . So let's look at the bird and see what it's doing—that's what counts. I learned very early the difference between knowing the name of something and knowing something."

Richard Feynman (1918–1988)

5

Practicum Supervision

"An education isn't how much you have committed to memory, or even how much you know. It's being able to differentiate between what you do know and what you don't."

Anatole France (1844–1924)

In her journal Marilyn made the following entry about her supervisor Joanne, a physical education teacher in a school for children with severe intellectual disability.

> *Joanne was always and still is available to answer any questions or concerns we have. She is a very open person, and I did not feel intimidated by her at all. She is respectful of the practicum students and the students in her class. She encourages us to get involved. At the beginning of each class she would point out anything important we needed to know about a specific child. After every class she asked for our opinions and suggestions. She gave us several opportunities to run the class. Joanne has a great sense of humor and is very enthusiastic. I enjoyed working with her.*

In chapter 1, we briefly described the many settings in which a practicum experience can take place, and it's fair to assume that similar types of learning will occur regardless of the setting. First, you'll have an opportunity to link practice to theory. Second, within the framework of structured placements you can test your knowledge, skills, and attitudes in a real-world workplace. Practicum also provides an opportunity to develop new competencies while identifying areas in which you feel you need further education and training.

Like Marilyn, if you're in a supervised practicum you'll also gain insights into professional practice. How much you learn might depend on the environment and the supervision you have in your placement. Keep this in mind when you start your practicum. You're entering a new learning environment in which you're expected to practice professional skills in adapted physical activity using the knowledge you're acquiring in your undergraduate courses. Marilyn's supervisor wanted to hear her opinions. However, she's not yet a professional, so she's fortunate to have regular and appropriate supervision. Whether you're embarking on your first practicum experience or have previously participated in a practicum, many things can help both you and the person who is supervising have the best possible experience.

Your supervisor is a critical component of your placement. He or she is a valuable learning resource.

Remember that a practicum is designed to be a learning experience for you. Usually the people who are supervising your practicum have, compared to you, a lot of practical experience. Their willingness to supervise implies that they're there to help you learn—so, think of your supervisor as a learning resource. He or she is a critical component of your placement. "Supervision which the student receives in the workplace is usually the most important factor in determining the quality of the experience" (Ryan, Toohey, & Hughes, 1996, p. 372). You can play a role in the ultimate outcome of your experience by ensuring that your supervisor gives you information that meets your needs. Your supervisor is there to offer support. Take the time to evaluate your personal feelings and share them with your supervisor. Be honest about your emotions—this will help you communicate more effectively with your supervisor. Think critically about your practices in the placement, and ask questions that help you address your concerns. Above all, ask questions when you don't understand.

Types of Supervision

In adapted physical activity practica, supervision might vary considerably depending on the location and type of practicum. Supervision might be one on one or occur in groups. Supervisors might work alongside you or choose to observe you from outside the activity. Alternatively, you might receive indirect supervision from your course instructor.

In the one-on-one model, the supervisor acts as a guide or mentor and plays a primary role in modeling professionalism while observing your practice and offering feedback. In group supervision, you're part of a group of students participating in the same experience with one supervisor. In this case your activities and evaluative reviews are more likely to occur in the presence of your peers. Such an arrangement has advantages and disadvantages. Although there are benefits to sharing experiences with others in similar situations and discussing topics, such as problem solving, within a circle of people engaged in the same practicum experience, this dynamic is clearly not as personal as a one-on-one meeting with your supervisor. In the observation-style practicum you would expect to be working within the context of assigned tasks during which your supervisor would purposefully observe and assess your work at pre-arranged times. This assessment would be followed by a meeting with your supervisor in which you would receive feedback. For experienced practicum students, this type of supervision offers greater independence. Some experts consider one on one the preferred type of supervision (Knight, 2001); others suggest that it's not the type of supervision but the quality of supervision that matters.

Sometimes placements occur under the supervision of a first-time supervisor. If this happens to you, it's up to you to inform the supervisor about your responsibilities and the requirements of the course. Also be sure to determine and understand your supervisor's expectations for you and the course. The following comments are a good example of a neophyte's perception of accepting a practicum student.

> The idea of a practicum student . . . was very attractive. At the onset, I thought that my time commitment would be about an hour a week. It was more like three hours a week. In retrospect, I think supervision time could have been reduced if I had front-loaded my work. However, Wendy and I were both learning—she in her role of practicum student and me in my role of supervisor. (Okahashi & Roby-Straza, 2002, p. 1)

Effective Supervision

You should expect confirmation during your practicum. From his research on the perceptions of a supervisor's role in regard to practicum students, Johnson (1987) concluded that students seek two distinct roles from a supervisor: evaluative feedback and support. Initially, practicum students look to their course instructor, but as the term proceeds they turn more frequently to the supervisor of the practicum for support and feedback (Johnson, 1986). Abramson and Fortune (1990) also found that support and feedback were the two factors most important to student satisfaction.

Your supervisor is someone who can answer many of your questions and give you helpful suggestions. Ideally, every practicum student receives an interim or formative evaluation. In some cases you'll receive periodic feedback from your supervisor throughout your practicum, but you should always receive feedback at the conclusion of your placement. In programs where direct supervision isn't available, your APA course instructor should be accessible for consultation and feedback on your activities.

Orientation

Ideally the atmosphere of your practicum is positive, goal oriented, and flexible. Whether your placement is at an agency, institution, community, or school, most well-established sites offer an orientation to the facility, services, and programs they offer. During this orientation you might expect to learn about the facility, their agency's philosophy of service delivery, their services and programs, the staff, and the people who use the facility. Most important, you should be informed about accident and emergency procedures and rules about access to information and confidentiality policies.

Practice Under Supervision

It's not easy to guide someone else's learning experience. One of the most important roles your supervisor can offer is to prompt you to question your underlying assumptions and beliefs while offering you the support you need to confidently fulfill your role as a practicum student. Rogers, Collins, Barlow, and Grinnel (2000) have identified a series of productive tensions embedded in the teaching and learning process. They describe these tensions in terms of opposing forces, including challenge versus support, openness versus defensiveness, risk taking versus safety, demand for work versus self-direction, autonomy versus dependency, moving forward versus staying the same, authority versus mutuality, learning objectives versus practicum setting's objectives, and education versus training. We'll look at each of these types of tension in the sections that follow.

Challenge Versus Support

Challenge helps you think critically; it helps you think of alternative ways of knowing and practicing. But it can also be threatening. Thus, you should think of a challenge as an opportunity to reflect on and analyze your behavior, whereas your supervisor should support you in a way that demonstrates sensitivity to your response to the challenges.

Jason's supervisor at the fitness center asked him to change Harry's program in a way that would make it more challenging for Harry. Someone else had set the routine before Jason arrived, and when Jason started they agreed to continue with the same program. That was six weeks earlier, and now the supervisor, Phil, was asking for a change. Jason knew exactly what to do, but for some reason he felt reluctant to introduce the changes to Harry. The following week, Phil talked to Jason before Harry arrived. Phil said that he sensed Jason was hesitant and wondered if he was concerned about how Harry would respond. He told Jason that he realized Jason knew what to do and how to do it, but that perhaps Jason was concerned that Harry might not be too happy with the changes. He asked Jason what he could do to help out. Jason felt relieved after their conversation, and he also thought about Phil's comments and realized that he was thinking more about himself than what would be best for Harry.

Openness Versus Defensiveness

We can all get defensive when our thinking or behavior is challenged, but it's healthy to be willing to consider new ideas or new ways of doing things. At the same time, your supervisor needs to avoid intimidation or undermining your confidence so that you can be open to new possibilities and options.

Suzanne was always animated and spoke a decibel or two above normal when she was working in an exercise program with elderly people with osteoarthritis. Her supervisor felt she was sending the message that all older people are deaf. After the class ended, she and Suzanne chatted. She complimented Suzanne on another great class and mentioned how much she admired her enthusiasm. She then asked if she would consider reducing the volume when she was talking to participants and concluded by saying, "You've got such terrific energy—it shows in the way you move and the attention you give everyone." Suzanne got the point and confidently thought about the next class, planning to speak a little more softly.

Risk Taking Versus Safety

Adopting new ways of thinking and behaving involves taking risks. You must be willing to take the risks, and your supervisor needs to create a safe environment in which you can transform your assumptions and beliefs.

Jason knew that by agreeing to change Harry's program, he risked losing Harry's support. Harry might feel he was being pushed unreasonably, or he might become frustrated and even stop coming. Phil, his supervisor, was reassuring and supportive, which allowed Jason to proceed with confidence and security.

Demand for Work Versus Self-Direction

You can increase your confidence by finding a balance between completing the work, tasks, and assignments your supervisor asks of you and directing your energy toward your own initiatives. Your supervisor and you should agree on the suitability of occasions for you to make decisions and follow through with appropriate action.

Sean's practicum was in a class that included children with attention-deficit hyperactivity disorder (ADHD). He found the physical education program was pretty standard and that he spent most of his time managing behavior. He felt that if the class could do a new activity that wasn't part of the standard curriculum, the students might be motivated to pay attention and concentrate. He wanted to take the class to a climbing wall. His supervisor was pleased to learn that Sean hadn't mentioned anything to the children yet, and he asked Sean to explain his idea. They ended the conversation with Sean agreeing to find out about costs, liability issues, and transportation options for a trip to the local climbing wall.

Autonomy Versus Dependency

Given an environment that supports self-direction, your supervisor should then balance the amount of direction that he or she provides with opportunities that allow you to work autonomously.

Sean was well versed in the strategies to keep participants on task and cooperating in the games unit. He was really pleased when the teacher arrived and asked Sean to get the class started while he worked with a couple of the students individually for the first 10 minutes.

Moving Forward Versus Staying the Same

Being challenged and supported in an environment in which you're given responsibility for decisions and the opportunity for making choices primes you for moving forward. It's up to you to demonstrate your readiness to take the next step. Again,

Your supervisor should give you opportunities to work autonomously with learners.

your supervisor has a supportive role to play. At times, staying the same can reinforce good learning. At other times, you'll be ready to move forward.

Near the end of the practicum Sean's supervisor asked him if he would be interested in returning for the next term. Sean considered his options. If he returned, he felt that based on his experience he would likely be given more responsibility, but he would be doing more of the same old thing. Alternatively, if he went to the middle school, he'd have a chance to work with older kids. However, in the middle school he wouldn't have much independence or responsibility.

Authority Versus Mutuality

Despite the many opportunities you might have to work independently, your supervisor is in a position of authority. He or she has the power to direct your activity and control all decisions. Good supervision takes into account the need for you as a student to assume a collaborative role on some occasions and a partnered or independent role on other occasions. The balance of these two will reinforce your growth and learning during the practicum.

Nicki was working with a group of competitive cyclists who are blind. She didn't agree with the training program their coach had set up for the athletes. She felt they would peak too soon for the upcoming meet. She was pleased that the coach was willing to discuss her concerns. In the end, however, he reinforced his commitment to his decisions and encouraged Nicki to work with him in preparing the team for the meet.

Learning Objectives Versus Practicum Setting's Objectives

Your supervisor is responsible to the organization or institution for which he or she works. At times, tension can develop between your supervisor's ability to meet the demands or goals of his or her employer and his or her ability to facilitate your educational objectives in a way that ensures your learning experiences match your program requirements. In such cases, take time to consider your supervisor's delicate position.

Lauren was concerned because she knew she was supposed to be participating in an inclusive physical education program, but she found that the teacher, Leslie, was constantly asking her to take Michelle, who uses an electric wheelchair, to a corner where she and Michelle could work together. Lauren wanted Michelle to be fully included in the class and felt frustrated that she wasn't. However, when Lauren thought about it, she realized Leslie might be concerned about Michelle's safety. She realized that Leslie had a large group and sometimes had to spend more time on organization than she would have liked. Lauren realized she wasn't going to get as much time in fully inclusive programming as she'd hoped, but she understood the importance of keeping all the learners safe and all activities organized.

Education Versus Training

Finally, a tension exists in striving for a balance between learning job-related tasks (training) and becoming educated in your chosen profession of adapted physical activity. During your time in your practicum, you'll want to develop skills as well as your knowledge base, understanding that at times the importance of one will outweigh the other. A good supervisor helps you achieve a balance.

Daphne really enjoyed the time that she and her supervisor spent together over coffee after her practicum at the community center. She and her supervisor got into great discussions about philosophical positions and theory in APA. This was stuff Daphne had seen in her textbook, but she found it dry and hard to read. These discussions brought the material to life and made her question the way she practiced APA.

Summary

Support from your supervisor is the key element of your practicum. He or she will broaden your professional perspective and help you develop new understandings of the theoretical information you're studying in your course. You won't have infinite access to your supervisor, so learn as much from him or her as you can while you have the opportunity.

Exercise 5.1
Goals

If you have a supervised practicum, write in your personal goals for the practicum in table 5.1 and compare them with those your supervisor has provided. If your practicum is unsupervised, write in your course instructor's goals.

1. Compare the two sets of goals. Are they similar? Are they different but compatible? In your opinion, are there changes that should be made to the goals set by either your instructor or your supervisor?

_____

_____

_____

_____

2. About halfway through your practicum, ask your supervisor, course instructor, or another appropriate person to provide you with an interim (formative) evaluation of your participation thus far. Let this person know that you'll be asking for another evaluation at the end of the practicum. Your evaluator might have a tool he or she prefers to use, but if not you can use tables 5.2 and 5.3 for your evaluation.

Table 5.1

Practicum Goals

Your goals	Your supervisor's goals	Your instructor's goals

Table 5.2

Sample Tool: Formative Evaluative Feedback

Practicum student:_____ Date:_____

Placement: _____

Skill	Evidence of effectiveness	Evidence of ineffectiveness	Suggestions
Organization (e.g., is on time; completes reports or forms as requested; brings appropriate materials to practicum)			
Professional skills (e.g., selects appropriate activities; implements safety procedures)			
Instructional skills (e.g., conveys clear instructions; adapts based on learner responses)			
Interaction with program participants; behavior management (e.g., speaks respectfully to participants; shows genuine interest in participants; reinforces appropriate behavior)			

Table 5.3

Summative (Final) Evaluation Feedback

Practicum student:_____ Date:_____

Placement: _____

Skill	Evidence of effectiveness	Evidence of ineffectiveness	Suggestions
Organization (e.g., is on time; completes reports or forms as requested; brings appropriate materials to practicum)			
Professional skills (e.g., selects appropriate activities; implements safety procedures)			
Instructional skills (e.g., conveys clear instructions; adapts based on learner responses)			
Interaction with program participants; behavior management (e.g., speaks respectfully to participants; shows genuine interest in participants; reinforces appropriate behavior)			

6

Learning Plans

"Perhaps the most valuable result of all education is the
ability to make yourself do the thing you have to do,
when it ought to be done, whether you like it or not;
it is the first lesson that ought to be learned;
and however early a man's training begins, it is probably
the last lesson that he learns thoroughly."

Thomas H. Huxley (1825–1895)

Frank came to college with a lot of high school basketball experience. While he was never a starter on the high school team, he loves the sport. He also knows what it's like to "ride the bench." He wants to help other kids learn basketball, but more than anything he wants them to enjoy the experience. He has enrolled in an APA course because he thinks his experience with high school basketball will be useful to kids whose skills and abilities make them vulnerable in regular physical education classes. His instructor places him in a high school after-school sports program in which there is a significant number of students who have been identified as having learning disabilities. The leader of the after-school program is frustrated with the numbers of kids in the program and with their lack of "motivation" and their physical awkwardness. He's hoping Frank can provide an extra set of hands to manage the kids. Frank's instructor wants Frank to develop some leadership skills and program-development skills. When Frank visits the program to get a sense of the physical environment, participants, and activities being offered, he's overwhelmed by all the expectations confronting him. How will he ever know what to do? Who will measure his success? After all, he needs a good grade in the class! But he really wants to help, and he remembers what it's like to sit out while everyone else is playing. After all, he's there for the kids, right?

The responsibility for learning through experience is jointly held. Your instructor has specific goals for you related to the course associated with the practicum. The agency or individual with whom you're working also has expectations. Finally, you have strengths that need to be used and needs that have to be met through the practicum for your development as a person and as a professional.

Frank felt a little overwhelmed. He didn't know where or how to start, but he had the right idea—he was thinking about the kids first. Getting yourself organized for learning in a practicum takes some planning.

The first step in developing your learning plan is to clearly understand the purpose of your practicum experience. What are the goals and objectives of the course you're taking? How does the practicum relate to these goals and objectives? This information should be specified in your course syllabus, which is the contract between you and your instructor. The practicum may have specific experiences and assignments associated with it. The syllabus should list these and include the weighting of the practicum and the evaluation criteria. If these are not clear, speak to your instructor and develop a mutual understanding regarding the practicum.

Frank reviewed his syllabus (course outline) and realized that he will learn many things in the course that will help him. More importantly, it reminded him that in the practicum he was still a student and he was expected to be learning in the practicum. No one expected him to have all the answers.

Example of course goals

1. To increase students' level of awareness regarding disability in society and the role of physical activity in the lives of people with disability
2. To facilitate experiential learning in adapted physical activity for each student, through an appropriate practicum placement

Examples of course objectives: Goal Two objectives

When they have completed the course, students should be able to do the following:

1. Discuss the importance of considering age-appropriateness when selecting activities for a program.
2. Describe the principles that guide adaptations for learning and participating in physical activities as they pertain to the APA practicum.

Agencies that support practicum placements expect students to behave professionally during all phases of the practicum. Professional behavior includes a positive self-regard, self-awareness, interpersonal competence, contribution to the learning of others, and a commitment to learning. In addition, the agency expects students to fulfill a role related to their skills, abilities, and knowledge. At the placement you might be given a job description that identifies whom to report to, training requirements, expectations regarding your time commitment, and a list of tasks.

A personal learning plan needs to take into account both the instructor's and the agency's expectations. Your plan should also include an assessment of your personal learning needs and your learning style. In chapter 1 we discussed your need to understand your values, attitudes, and expertise. You completed several exercises that helped you clarify your values and identify your strengths that must be taken into account in developing your learning plan. In this chapter you'll complete exercises to assist you in learning more about your learning style.

Learning Styles

Your learning style indicates your preferences for learning and can be understood from a couple of perspectives. For example, preferences can be viewed according to sensory modality—that is, visual, auditory, or tactile/kinesthetic. The visual learner gains knowledge most effectively through seeing. Effective teaching strategies for the visual learner include modeling, visual displays, and observation of the instructor's

Visual learners gain knowledge most effectively through seeing, so employ strategies for visual learners such as modeling and visual displays.

body language and instruction. Auditory learners learn best through listening. Verbal lectures, discussions, and talking things through are of most benefit to auditory learners. Tactile or kinesthetic learners learn best through moving, doing, and touching. They like a hands-on approach and active exploration of the world around them. Most people are visual learners (about 60 percent), but auditory learners (30 percent) and tactile or kinesthetic learners (10 percent) are also quite common. See the Web site www.academictips.org/memory/mnemlsty.html for more information on learning styles.

Another perspective of learning style is Kolb's Learning Style Inventory (1984), which identifies four fundamental learning styles. In chapter 2 we discussed how learning style influences the way you write in your journal. In this chapter we'll explore how your preferred learning style influences how you acquire knowledge and the strategies that support different learning styles.

Kolb considered learning style as a continuum that moves from concrete experience through reflective observation and abstract conceptualization to active experimentation. However, most learners prefer one of the styles above the others. The four styles are described according to learner types, which include divergers, assimilators, convergers, and accommodators.

Divergers prefer to acquire information through concrete experience. They rely on their feelings and have a need to express those feelings while they learn. As a diverger you will shine in the practicum because personal interaction is another key to your learning preference. Not only do you have the opportunity for interaction while working with participants in the practicum, you can also seek opportunities to discuss the practicum with your supervisor. You can see things from different perspectives and are good at generating new ideas, which you enjoy sharing in discussions with others.

Using the diverger approach, you're encouraged to

- try out adapted equipment and explore new ways to use it;
- ask "Why?" to aid your understanding of tactics and concepts associated with your practicum; and
- talk to your peers about your practice, seeking their response to your ideas.

Assimilators prefer to reflect and observe. They seek information, including what the experts think, through reading and listening. If you're an assimilator, you'll analyze, organize, and assimilate pieces of information to arrive at a complete picture. Even though you're detail oriented, you like to develop a conceptual picture. In the practicum you'll get along well with your supervisor because of your strong organizational skills. You'll also likely be admired for your willingness to take direction and your ability to follow instructions accurately and efficiently.

Using the assimilator approach, you're encouraged to

- take the time to observe during your initial stages of the practicum;
- reflect on the practicum experience, refer to resource materials, and summarize your experience; and
- consider ways in which the practicum could be better organized.

Convergers prefer to learn by doing. They like to test information, to try things out for themselves. They are interested primarily in the reality of the practicum rather than the theory or information they've studied in class. They're concerned about the practicality of a situation and thus enjoy practicum activities that have strong relevance to the goals of a program. If you're a converger, you can make decisions quickly and prefer to deal only with essential information. Not surprisingly, you tend to like to work alone. Your strength in the practicum is your ability to work with minimum supervision and recognize changes and modifications that could improve the practicum experience.

Using the converger approach, you're encouraged to

- volunteer for practicum tasks that allow you to work independently;
- review resources and identify key concepts and essential elements to assist you in practice; and
- during your evaluation, identify ways that the practicum placement could be modified to improve the experience for future students.

Accommodators prefer independent discovery. They are motivated by taking information and creating something new. If you're an accommodator, you'll like finding your own way, and you might resent a practicum situation in which there are extensive rules and procedures. Further, because you're a problem solver and a risk taker, you like to explore and learn from your mistakes. You're happiest when your supervisor is there for you but doesn't hover over you. Given this preference, you must take care not to try new things without approval. Your love of teaching will produce good results during your practicum, and you'll accomplish a lot with your students.

Using the accommodator approach, you're encouraged to

- identify problems and take advantage of the opportunity to find new solutions;
- talk to your peers and explain or discuss the problems you've solved; and
- request approval from your practicum supervisor before trying a new approach to an exercise or activity.

You might recognize your learning preferences in more than one or perhaps all the descriptions of learner types. Because Kolb originally described these styles as part of a continuum, this is not surprising. However, most people feel a stronger affinity to one of the types over the others. Learning more about your learning style preference allows you to use your strengths to improve your practicum experience. At the end of the chapter is an exercise to help you determine which learner type you most resemble (exercise 6.1).

Multiple Intelligences

Gardner (1993) posed the idea that people express intellectual abilities in different ways. Based on multiple intelligence (MI) theory, he describes seven different ways of learning that are characterized by seven intelligences: visual–spatial, verbal–linguistic, logical–mathematical, body–kinesthetic, musical–rhythmic, interpersonal, and intrapersonal.

- **Visual–spatial intelligence** is the ability to perceive the visual. Information is stored in mental images. Visual–spatial intelligence is displayed through puzzle building, writing, manipulating images and objects, and creating visual metaphors to represent reality.

- **Verbal–linguistic intelligence** is the ability to use words and language. This includes expression through writing, storytelling, speaking, and analyzing language use.

- **Logical–mathematical intelligence** is the ability to use reason, logic, and numbers. Best seen as the ability to perceive patterns and connections among pieces of information, this intelligence emphasizes active experimentation with ideas.

- **Body–kinesthetic intelligence** is displayed through controlled body movements and skillful handling of objects. Motor skills are refined, and the body is used actively in problem solving.

- **Musical–rhythmic intelligence** is the ability to produce and appreciate movement. Through thinking in sounds, rhythms, and patterns, learners produce and perform music and express themselves through music.

- **Interpersonal** and **intrapersonal intelligence** both involve the ability to relate to others and understand yourself. Interpersonal abilities—including empathy and communication—let you see things from another's point of view. Intrapersonal intelligence allows you to be self-reflective and aware of your inner self. At the end of this chapter (exercise 6.2), you're directed to a Web site at which you can complete a test that determines which of the seven strengths you're likely to apply most often.

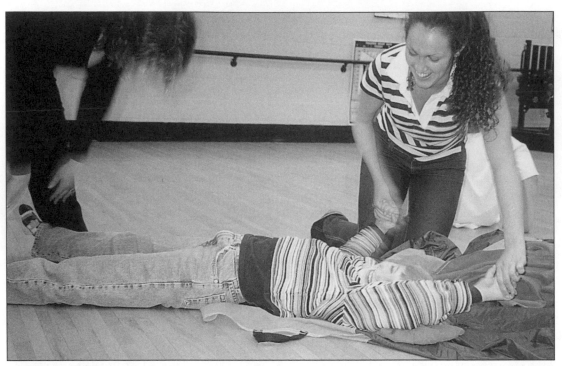

One of the seven ways of learning in multiple intelligence theory is body–kinesthetic intelligence. Body–kinesthetic intelligence is displayed through controlled body movements and skillful handling of objects.

Learning Map

Reaching your objectives for your practicum requires a plan. Think of the process you use when you're preparing for a long road trip. First you determine where you want to go—your goal or destination. Next, you look at a map and identify how to break the trip into manageable pieces—your stops along the way. Each piece brings you closer to your goal. Each time you stop you can review your plan and make adjustments—change your route, spend more time in certain places, and so on. You'll increase your chances of reaching your goal in your practicum if you view it as you would a road trip. After all, your practicum is a journey.

When your instructor decided to include a practicum as part of your course, he or she probably developed some goals and objectives from his or her perspective. You also need to develop your own goals and objectives that are congruent with the instructor's practicum objectives.

Identifying Your Learning Objectives

Your objectives are the map for your practicum. They convey your orientation to the practicum and are based on your philosophy, values, skills, and abilities. Your goals should be congruent with the goals and objectives your instructor has set for the practicum and with the roles and responsibilities the agency has determined are part of your job.

The process begins with reviewing what you know. Information and activities from earlier chapters have helped you determine and assess your values, beliefs, strengths, and weaknesses. This assessment and your knowledge of the practicum provide the framework. After reviewing these, you need to brainstorm to find your goals and objectives areas, which might fall within the cognitive, affective, or psychomotor domains.

Next, determine how appropriate these areas are for your practicum. Can you achieve your goals and objectives in the time you've allotted for the practicum? Will your roles and responsibilities in the agency allow you to work toward the achievement of your objectives? Are the areas congruent with the goals and objectives of the course?

Objectives can be written from two perspectives: (1) what you want to accomplish to meet your needs and (2) what you will provide to the people with disability with whom you're working. Objectives are specific. They identify what you want to accomplish, set a time frame, and describe an outcome. For example, you might want to learn how to transfer a person from a wheelchair to a swimming pool. If so, your objective might be, *After training by my instructor, I will transfer my client from his or her manual wheelchair to the mechanical lift using a one-person, stand–pivot transfer with verbal cues from my instructor.* Similarly, the person you're working with might have as a goal, "I want to learn how to swim." To help him or her learn how to swim, you'll need to break the goal into smaller pieces: objectives. One of your objectives for this student might be, "After verbal instruction and demonstration, Gerald will place his face in the water and blow bubbles." These sample objectives are missing some pieces that you'll learn about later in this chapter.

As your thinking level and your understanding increase during your practicum, the language and words you use will change. The changes in your goals and objectives will be reflected in this new language.

Creating Objectives

Goals and objectives are made meaningful by the words that create them. Appropriate words for creating objectives can be drawn from Bloom's taxonomy.

Cognitive Domain

Bloom (1956) suggests that the cognitive domain includes a continuum of cognitive processes that require increasing skills and abilities. He lists the following processes of cognition from simplest to most difficult: knowledge, comprehension, application, analysis, synthesis, and evaluation (see figure 6.1). *Knowledge* indicates that a person knows something in the sense that he or she can repeat the information that has been learned. Bloom suggests that listing, matching, naming, and defining are among the objectives that someone with knowledge might strive for. *Comprehension* indicates an understanding and might include objectives such as developing one's ability to describe, give examples, and summarize. *Application* implies that information can be used in practical situations. Objectives might involve one's ability to change, predict, or solve. *Analysis* involves the ability to take something apart, to understand its components. Objectives might include developing skills in discrimination, inference, and appropriate selection. *Synthesis* is the process of putting things together or back together in new ways. Objectives would involve designing, reorganizing, and modifying. *Evaluation* refers to the ability to form a judgment and determine how well a concept works for a particular

TIP Bloom's processes are based on the theory that knowledge is necessary before comprehension. You must be able to list the parts of an objective before you can summarize and describe what an objective is. Don't forget that motivation plays a strong part in moving through these cognitive processes.

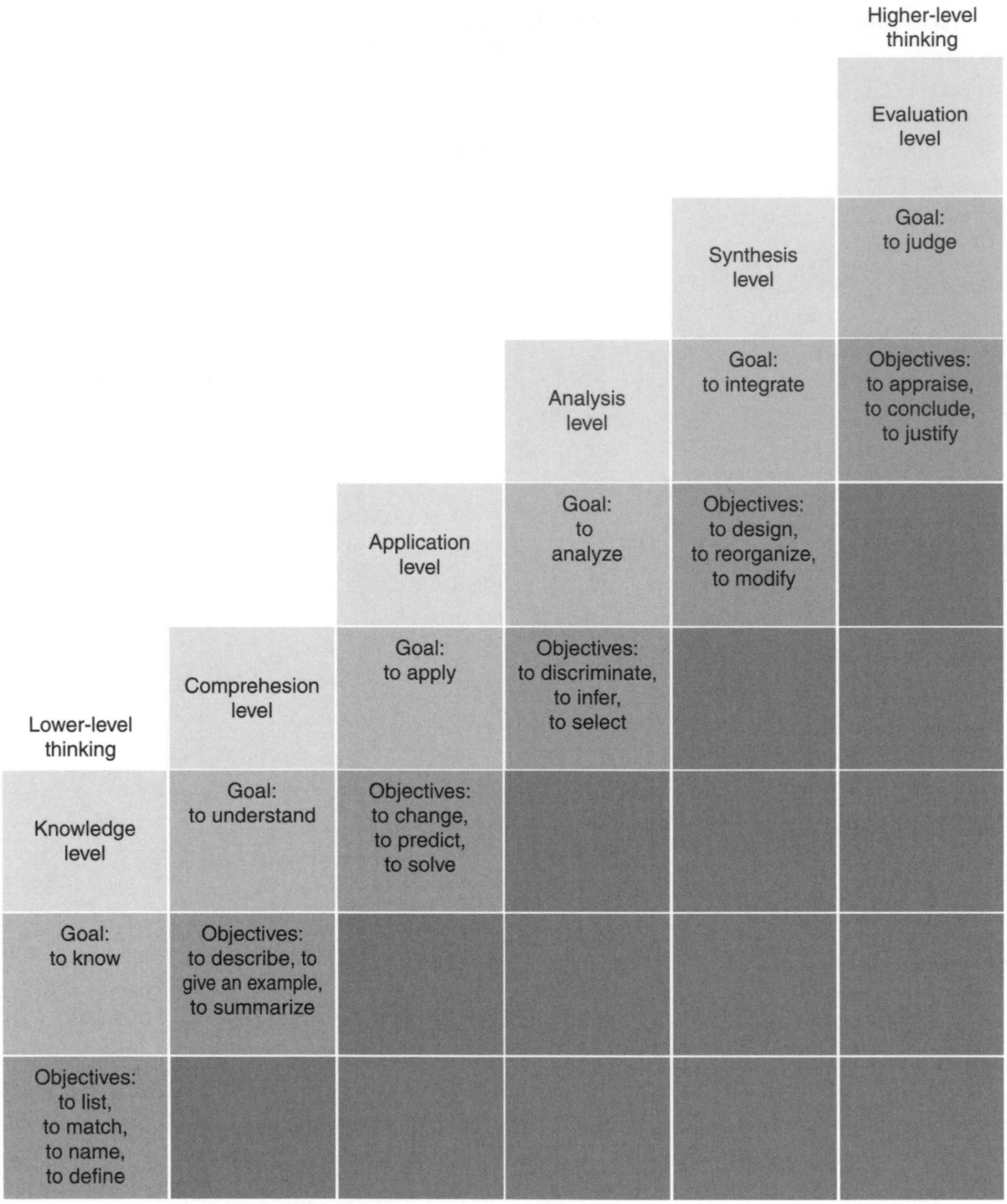

Higher-level thinking

				Evaluation level
			Synthesis level	Goal: to judge
		Analysis level	Goal: to integrate	Objectives: to appraise, to conclude, to justify
	Application level	Goal: to analyze	Objectives: to design, to reorganize, to modify	
Comprehesion level	Goal: to apply	Objectives: to discriminate, to infer, to select		

Lower-level thinking

Knowledge level	Goal: to understand	Objectives: to change, to predict, to solve		
Goal: to know	Objectives: to describe, to give an example, to summarize			
Objectives: to list, to match, to name, to define				

Figure 6.1 Goals and objectives grouped by levels of Bloom's Taxonomy Educational Objectives.

From *Learning Skills for College and Career* 2nd edition by HETTICH. © 1998. Reprinted with permission of Wadsworth, a division of Thomson Learning: www.thomsonrights.com. Fax 800-730-2215.

situation. Objectives might involve appraising, drawing conclusions, and reaching justifications.

Affective Domain

Changes in your thinking will be reflected in your feelings and beliefs. Krathwohl, Bloom, and Masia (1964) describe the taxonomy of educational objectives in the affective domain according to receiving, responding, valuing, organizing, and characterizing.

Try the following words in the affective domain:

Listens	Shows sensitivity
Attends	Receives
Responds	Obeys, completes, volunteers, enjoys
Values	Believes, appreciates
Organizes	Recognizes, formulates
Characterizes	Displays, practices, uses

Psychomotor Domain

The psychomotor domain focuses on observable behaviors in the form of movement and actions. Bush (1972) offers the following words that reflect objective behaviors in this domain: "imitates," "manipulates," "accuracy and control of errors" (precision), "articulation" (coordination of tasks), and "naturalization" (part of a routine, automatic, spontaneous).

TIP Similar to the cognitive domain, these psychomotor skills are built on the concept of a continuum. Before physical skills can become automatic and part of a routine, the person first learns to demonstrate the skills.

Your selection of words is significant because objectives need to be clear, measurable, behavioral, functional, and appropriate to your needs. "Clear" means that the objective must be understandable. Use words that make sense to you. To be measurable, the objective must be written to describe a performance, the conditions of the performance, and the quality or level of performance expected. Performance-based objectives are also behavioral. "Functional" and "appropriate to your needs" indicate that the objectives should relate to your abilities to perform in an everyday environment that's important to you.

To write an objective, write a sentence such as this one. A suggested format is: _____ (name) will _____ (the behavior) _____ (the conditions) _____ (the criteria or level of the performance) by _____ (date). An example might be: Beth (the performer) will accurately demonstrate a stand–pivot transfer from a wheelchair to a desk chair (the behavior) twice (the criteria or level of the performance) without assistance (the conditions) by March 15 (date).

Identifying Your Learning Plan

A learning plan includes more than your assessment and objectives. The plan needs to identify the resources at your disposal to accomplish the plan, the methods and environment required, the frequency and duration of your practicum placement, and a plan for evaluation.

Resource identification is an important piece of your plan. Typical resources available include your instructors, other students, the people to whom you're providing services, the agency staff, the Internet, your social support system, your textbooks, services at your university, and college and community agencies.

In addition to knowledge resources, you need to consider financial resources. Will your instructor, educational institution, or the agency for which you're working provide you with a budget? What will the budget cover? For example, can you buy program materials, pay for transportation, or pay participant fees from the budget?

The methods you'll use to achieve your objectives are critical to your success. Take into account your learning style and the concept of multiple intelligence. How and where do you learn best? How much of a discrepancy is there between where you are now and the outcomes of your objectives? What types of formal methods (reading a chapter from a textbook) and informal methods (discussing and reflecting on an experience with others) will you use to achieve your objectives?

How long do you have to achieve your objectives? The frequency and duration of your practicum put practical limits on your achievements. If you provide service once a week for one hour each time over 10 weeks, you'll address different needs than you will in two days of five hours each.

Finally, what methods of evaluation will you use? Identify the format and structure that your agency or instructor prefers. It might be a standardized assessment with an accompanying form or an agency-developed evaluation process. Or you might be asked to develop your own method of evaluation. Regardless, you might receive input for your evaluation from your own reflections, feedback from your agency supervisor, input from those you work with, contributions from other students, and comments from your course instructor.

In summary, your learning plan will include goals to determine what you want to accomplish in your practicum, objectives to help you get there, and a method for determining how well you did. To be successful, you and those you work with will take into account your learning style and take advantage of your multiple intelligences.

Identify Your Role in Achieving the Program Learning Plan

To implement your learning plan you need to clearly identify your role and the roles of your course instructor and agency supervisor. Develop at least a verbal contract, and ideally a written contract, that states who's responsible for developing the practicum, contracting with the practicum site, determining and maintaining legal requirements, administering the practicum program, and administering the evaluation process. What training will you receive and when will it occur?

TIP ▷ This is your personal learning plan for your practicum. It doesn't apply to the people you work with—it's all about you!

For each objective, identify what you will have to do to meet the objective. What supports will you need, and how will you get them? Finally, how do your roles as learner and service provider integrate?

Clarify Expectations

For a successful experience, make sure you know the agency requirements regarding arriving late, being absent, and making up time. Clarify what records you need to keep. Is there a time sheet to complete? Do you record interactions with clients in a book? What is your role in an emergency?

Summary

A practicum is an opportunity to apply classroom learning in the real world. Health conditions become real people. But because the practicum involves real people, it's imperative that you clearly understand your roles, responsibilities, and expectations. A practicum is more than a service opportunity—it's intended to be a learning experience.

Learning Style Preferences

In table 6.1, attributes of Kolb's Learning Styles Inventory are listed. Beside the listed terms, cite examples of your learning behavior that reflect evidence that you learn in this way. At the conclusion of this exercise pick the style that best describes your learning preferences.

Table 6.1
Learning Styles

Learning styles	Evidence of your preferences

Diverger
    Relevancy is important
    Asks, "Why are we doing this?"
    Needs personal interaction
    Learns through discussion
    Sees different perspectives
    Generates new ideas	

Assimilator
    Information is important
    Likes detail, directions, and order
    Likes to analyze and synthesize
    Learns by reading and listening
    Summarizes well	

Converger
    Learning by doing is important
    Makes decisions quickly
    Prefers to work alone
    Likes practicality
    Interested in the "how"
    Cuts to essentials quickly	

Accommodator
    Likes to find his or her own way
    Takes information and creates
      something new
    Problem solver
    Risk taker
    Likes to learn from mistakes
    Good at adapting	

Your learning style preference: _____

Multiple Intelligences

Visit a Web site that includes an assessment of multiple intelligences. Some examples include the following sites. Complete an assessment of multiple intelligences.

http://surfaquarium.com/MI/index.htm

www.ldrc.ca/projects/miinventory/miinventory.php

(Typing "multiple intelligence" into your Web search engine will reveal additional sites.)

TIP Everyone has all intelligences. These tests reveal your strengths and preferences. In discussing the results, describe how well the assessment represents you by giving some examples that support your opinion.

Review the description of multiple intelligences. Record your results and then write one paragraph that summarizes how accurately the assessment "multiple intelligences" represents you.

_____

_____

_____

_____

Exercise 6.3
Learning Plan

Complete the following learning plan.

TIP Identify the skills, abilities, knowledge, values, and beliefs that relate directly to your performance in your practicum.

Name:_____ Date: _____

Course:_____ Agency:_____

Assessment

Skills and abilities:

_____

_____

_____

Knowledge:

_____

_____

_____

Values and beliefs:

_____

_____

_____

Learning style/multiple intelligence:

_____

_____

_____

Objectives: Cognitive Domain

(For example: "I will list each exercise for Jarod's rehabilitation program and describe the reasons that each exercise is part of his routine.")

1. _____

2. _____

3. _____

Resources

(For example: Jarod, Jarod's physiotherapist, my textbook, and the *Rehabilitation for Brain Injury Society*)

1. _____

2. _____

3. _____

Objectives: Affective Domain

(For example: "I will remember something that Jarod tells me from each session and ask him about it the following week.")

1. _____

2. _____

3. _____

Resources

(For example: "Write things Jarod tells me in my journal each week.")

1. _____

2. _____

Objectives: Psychomotor Domain

(For example: "I will learn Jarod's exercises and perform his routine with the same number of repetitions and at the same pace.")

1. _____

2. _____

Resources

(For example: my APA instructor, Jarod's physiotherapist, my exercise therapy textbook)

1. _____

2. _____

3. _____

Methods

(For example: Study Jarod's exercise file. Practice his exercise routine. Research brain injury in my textbook, on the Web, and through our local society for brain injury.)

1. Write down questions to ask Jarod, my supervisor, and the physiotherapist.

_____

_____

_____

_____

7

Assessment Tools

> **"Treat people as though they are what they ought to be and you help them become what they are capable of being."**
>
> Goethe (1749–1832)

Jennifer has just arrived at the Boys and Girls Club after-school program. She will be working with a 10-year-old girl named Erin who has cerebral palsy. Erin wants to take part in the gymnastics activities. Jennifer's APA instructor and the Boys and Girls Club gymnastics leader believes that Erin can participate, but they're not sure how—nor do they have a sense of what gymnastics activities need modification. It's Jennifer's job to perform an assessment so that Erin's participation will be successful. In Jennifer's cabinet of resources she has standardized assessments of motor function and cognitive function. She also has a sense of the gymnastics activities because she was a gymnast during her high school years. From her personal experience she has completed informal activity analyses. How can she make sure she really understands Erin's performance capacity, motivation, learning abilities, and interest in gymnastics? What tools might she use in her assessment? How will she know where to start?

Assessment has various connotations and purposes. Results of assessments of individual performance are used in placement decisions, program development, and the determination of appropriate environments in which the learner might participate.

Assessment involves testing, measuring, and evaluating individual performance and environmental support systems. The assessment process is ongoing and thus will likely occur more than once during your practicum work with an individual or group. Initially, assessment is completed to identify a learner's present level of performance. Assessment is also done during the delivery of a program—this is a formative assessment to determine an individual's progress toward reaching his or her goals. Summative assessment occurs at the end of your program to determine the effectiveness of the activities in helping the learner accomplish the goals he or she has set.

Assessing the Compatibility Between Person and Activity

The method of assessment depends on the data being collected. For example, an assessment of motor performance might test and measure the time it takes to complete a task. Attitudes are also important during the assessment process. You hope to see self-efficacy in participants, which is the belief that they can do (or learn to do) a task in an acceptable manner. Cognitive skills also come into play in psychomotor activities. For example, does the learner know the rules for the activity? In the area of motor performance assessment, there's some disagreement about what kind of information is important to gain. There are basically two schools of thought: the developmental approach and the task-specific approach. The developmental approach addresses how the individual compares to a typically developing person. In assessing a child within this view, information about reflex behaviors, sensory systems, motor patterns, and motor skills are compared to typical individuals of the same age. In the task-specific approach, motor patterns and movement skills in the areas of strength, endurance, flexibility, agility, speed, basic locomotion, and fine motor skills are assessed relative to the requirements of a specific task. These assessments are frequently criterion-reference–based on a task or activity analysis.

Journal entry from the early stages of a student's placement:

> After what I saw today, my beliefs have definitely changed, and I realize the importance of re-evaluating objectives and not creating them until a full assessment has been made. Assumptions are something that should be disregarded when working with people with disability; it doesn't take long to learn there are far more things that can be achieved than cannot be achieved.

In the abilities-based approach to service delivery the main concern is to create compatibility between the person and the activity he or she wishes to pursue. Choosing an activity can be difficult. Assessing compatibility might lead to a better choice of activities when planning a program. To begin, assess a person's functional abilities in relation to the functional requirements of an activity and the objectives for achievement relative to that activity. Abilities are described within six categories: mobility, object manipulation, cognitive function, communication and perception, behavior and social skills, and fitness (Longmuir, 2003).

Mobility is the ability to move from place to place. It relies primarily on gross motor skills such as walking, running, hopping, or jumping. At different stages of our lives we have different levels of the same ability. For example, a toddler will walk with a wide base of support and arms held out to the side. A very old person might walk with a shuffling gait. Alternatively, mobility might also be achieved through the use of mobility devices such as a wheelchair, walker, crutches, or scooter.

Different activities require different forms and levels of mobility. The game of sledge hockey requires the ability to move in an aluminum sled by propelling it with handheld sledge sticks that have picks on one end. Track events, on the other hand, require you to move as quickly as possible (e.g., running with a prosthesis or with a sighted guide or using a wheelchair) from the start to the finish line. The type of activity not only affects mobility requirements but also the level of performance; recreational participation usually requires considerably less skill than elite competition.

Object manipulation refers to the participant's ability to control or manipulate equipment. The interaction between the participant and equipment is fundamental to most physical activities. Object manipulation depends primarily on upper limb movement, coordination, and skills such as throwing, catching, or hitting. However, other activities (e.g., soccer) rely primarily on the use of other body parts for object manipulation. The use of modified equipment or "low tech" solutions such as straps or tape can significantly enhance the participant's ability to grasp, hold, control, and manipulate objects. For example, someone with a weak grasp might benefit from Velcro straps on hand pedals when using an arm ergometer for strength and endurance workouts.

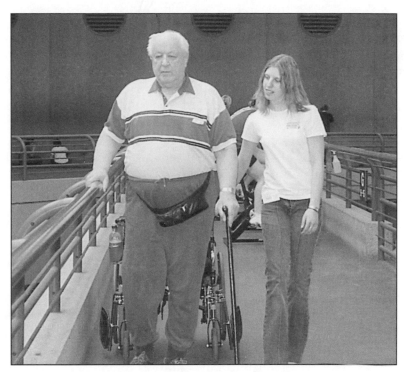

Mobility is one of the categories of abilities you must consider in an abilities-based approach to service delivery.

An impairment that affects object manipulation might result from paralysis (a lack of movement) or changes in movement speed, strength, or coordination. Object manipulation should be assessed based on the activity and adaptations made accordingly. For example, you can use a beach ball instead of a volleyball or a beanbag instead of a ball for catching and throwing.

Cognitive function encompasses all of a participant's mind functions, such as knowledge, understanding, memory, learning, association, and thinking. Cognitive function affects many abilities, such as a person's understanding of an activity's demands, learning of new activities, recalling activities previously learned, making decisions in response to changes in the activity's setting, and performing activities in an appropriate manner. Although cognitive function is commonly related to intellectual capacity, intelligence is but one aspect of cognitive function. Individuals with brain injuries might have a normal intellectual capacity but be unable to remember previous events. Learning disabilities, such as dyslexia, affect perception and might influence the ability to understand instructions or learn new skills. Different activities have different cognitive demands. For example, a team game such as basketball requires the ability to remember plays and a series of rules, whereas an activity such as swimming might only require knowing to stay in a particular lane.

Communication and perception abilities include an individual's capacity for interacting with the environment. These abilities rely primarily on sensory perceptions to convey information about the environment to the individual and on verbal and nonverbal communication skills to convey information from the individual to others in the environment. Communication and perception can be influenced by impairments of either the individual's receptive or expressive abilities. For example, individuals who can hear only loud sounds might have difficulty receiving auditory information but might be able to clearly express their own thoughts or needs through verbal communication. Conversely, individuals with aphasia (lack of speech) could easily hear and understand verbal instructions but might need to communicate their own thoughts and needs through nonverbal methods. The demand for communication abilities varies considerably depending on the activity. Team sports usually require quick and frequent verbal and nonverbal communication among players, whereas individual activities, such as swimming, running, or walking, require very little verbal communication.

Behavior and social skills influence the ability to perform an activity in the expected manner. These skills might also affect the interaction between the participant and instructor or other individuals. Disabilities related to behavior and social skills might result from conditions involving cognitive or emotional impairments. For many activities, variations in behavior don't significantly influence successful participation. For other activities, such as scuba diving or rock climbing, appropriate behavior is necessary for the safety of participants. Any individual, with or without a disability, might display inappropriate behavior or social skills. Don't accept or excuse inappropriate behavior just because the individual has a disability. But when correcting inappropriate behavior, focus on the behavior, not on the person.

The final category is *fitness*. Traditionally, the term "fitness" has been associated with changes in physiological measures of performance such as endurance, strength, and flexibility. The abilities-based approach defines fitness much more broadly, encompassing all the abilities required to sustain participation for the duration of the activity. For some activities, such as cross-country skiing, endurance measures of fitness might be the most relevant. For other activities, such as a personal training program, an individual's "fitness" might be defined psychologically in terms of ability to maintain concentration, commitment, or motivation. For example, cross-country skiing requires cardiovascular endurance, whereas archery requires the ability to concentrate for sustained periods. In a general sense, a person's fitness for an activity determines his or her ability to continue the activity from beginning to end.

The functional abilities required by an activity are evaluated using the six categories just identified: mobility, object manipulation, cognition, communication and perception, behavior and social skills, and fitness. Abilities-based assessment requires a clear understanding of all of the abilities' demands of an activity. These will vary among different activities and for the same activity depending on the setting or type of program. For example, mobility requirements vary significantly from activity to activity. Some activities require high speed or agility (e.g., track events), and others require very slow movements or virtually no mobility (e.g., tai chi or weight lifting). The focus of a physical activity program can also affect the mobility requirements for an activity. Consider the difference in mobility required for a stroke-improvement swim program compared to a competitive swim team.

Evaluating functional abilities required by an activity can be accomplished fairly quickly using observational techniques. Results from the person's functional assessment and the requirements of an activity are then compared. A level of the compatibility match is then determined and reviewed by the stakeholders (student, parent, volunteer, or teacher). In exercise 7.1 at the end of this chapter you'll be asked to complete a compatibility match for the individuals you're working with in your practicum. Decisions about the choice of a program or an activity can be made on the basis of this functional assessment. Successful participation or progress in the activity or program will require different types of assessment. At the end of this chapter is an exercise that gives you the opportunity to complete an observational functional assessment. This assessment process reviews functional abilities of the person as well as the requirements of the activity.

Formal and Informal Assessment

Formal assessments are typically standardized. They contain instructions that include a script for the evaluator to read and standardized instruments for data collection. They focus on isolated skills and are often used for eligibility and placement decisions. Formal assessments include developmental measures and tests that are standardized and norm referenced. Galagan (1985) indicates that standardized tests (a) are frequently culturally and socially biased, resulting in misclassification of minority children; (b) are often unreliable and invalidated for the purpose of determining which children have mild disabilities; (c) foster the creation of a dual education system; and (d) offer little or no direction for planning instruction.

Informal assessments include criterion-referenced tests in which a person's performance is compared to preselected criteria that measure mastery of a skill. These tests are usually closely matched to everyday tasks. If these are administered in contrived environments, the informal assessments might not tell you much about how the person functions under authentic conditions, in his or her natural environment. When possible, administer informal assessments in the environment that closely matches the setting in which the individual typically performs the task.

Assessment techniques include informal observations, reviews of history and records, and interviews. For observations to be useful as assessments, it's important to identify criteria for the observer to use. These could include parameters such as independence, safety, adequacy, and quality. Quality of performance parameters are shown by looking at such criteria as difficulty of performance, pain during or after performance, fatigue or dyspnea (shortness of breath) during or after performance, and duration of task performance.

Inventories are another type of informal assessment. These typically include a list (inventory) of skills needed to do a task. The skills are checked off as they are exhibited. Unfortunately, this procedure doesn't allow the evaluator a precise way to identify when parts of a skill are present but are weak or inadequate.

Informal assessments can be problematic because they have unclear directions for administration and nonstandardized instruments; they might also lack sensitivity to detect changes in people with special needs. Other areas to consider include the societal standards for performance. These standards are often referenced to culture, performer age and gender, and developmental level. It's also important to understand the performer's satisfaction with his or her performance and the perception of the experience. Finally, consider the resources available to support performance. These include accommodations such as adaptive equipment, level of social support, physical environment, financial considerations, and specialized support services such as the use of a personal aid.

Assessments can look at the differences among individuals or can reflect the level of individual growth. In any case, assessments should be truthful, trustworthy, and applicable to the person and his or her needs.

Authentic Assessment

Traditional assessment approaches in adapted physical activity often lead to frustrating experiences and questionable results because the tests are designed for a population without disability, or they are modifications of such tests. This has led to a growing shift toward using authentic assessment, which addresses a person's skills and abilities in a real-world setting (Wiggins, 1989). Authentic assessment uses performance samples to collect information on a person's competence at doing everyday activities and in using motor skills and abilities in functional tasks. Authentic assessment also assesses learning achievements in physical activity skills for games and recreational pursuits. In authentic assessments, performance is assessed according to a person's ability to use skills in a variety of authentic environments—physical places and situations that are part of the individual's everyday life experience. The assessment is linked to outcomes important to both the participant and the instructor. Assessments have a sense of authenticity because they require observation of a real-world performance. According to Winnick (2000), formal assessments and authentic assessments are not mutually exclusive. They can be used together and complement each other, gathering different types of information for a holistic picture of performance.

Direct observation of a participant requires that the observer take notes on behaviors that determine levels of competence or achievements. These notes are anecdotal records and narrative statements about significant behaviors, performance, or actions. Including the strategies used to accomplish the activity or motor behavior being demonstrated makes these notes more useful. They should also reflect any patterns that have developed in terms of approaching a task. The participant's comments and feedback add richness to the data and should also be recorded.

Self-assessment is an important component of authentic assessment. Self-assessment allows an individual to evaluate his or her own participation process and product of performance. This helps build understanding and insight of one's own performance abilities. Authentic assessments involve input and performance ratings from a variety of others, including teachers, peer reviewers, significant others, and coaches.

Authentic assessments can accommodate an individual's learning style and are oriented toward addressing multiple intelligences. However, they can be time consuming to develop because they require skills in task analysis; clarity in goals, outcomes, criteria, and expectations; and assurance that all stakeholders understand the assessment (Custer, Schell, McAlister, Scott, & Hoepfl, 2000). Among the characteristics of good authentic assessments are the following (Custer, 1994; Rudner & Boston, 1994):

• **Engaging, meaningful, worthy problems or tasks that match the content and outcomes of instruction.** For example, John, who uses a wheelchair and wants to improve his fitness, would participate in a program with content to match his needs—for example, strengthening upper body muscles used in transfers.

• **Real-life applicability.** Continuing with the previous example, the context or environment should be similar to that available elsewhere in the community. Accommodations to equipment should be minimal.

• **Multistaged demonstrations of knowing, knowing why, and knowing how.** What the participant has learned about fitness should be transferable to different pieces of equipment, different fitness facilities, and different environments (e.g., swimming pool and fitness center).

• **Emphasis on product and process, conveying that both development and achievement matter.** While learning how to lift weights, John learns about the importance of body position, full versus partial range of motion, and controlling the speed of flexion and extension during the lifting movement.

• **Rich, multidimensional, varied formats, both on demand and cumulative.** Here's an example of an on-demand assessment: "John, let me introduce you to Jarod. He's new to the program today. Can you show him the key points to remember when you do arm curls on this machine?" A cumulative assessment might include a portfolio of snapshots of John that illustrates at least one key point for each exercise in his program.

• **Opportunities for the learner to showcase achievement and do self-evaluation.** Videotaping John during selected exercises and then comparing his performance to an expert on tape is one way of creating opportunities for self-evaluation. You could also ask him to keep a journal about his workouts, including comments about his feelings and perceptions about his achievements.

• **Cognitive complexity, requiring higher-order thinking skills.** For example, John uses a wheelchair in a weight-training class, so the skills he should learn include the following: the transfers he uses in getting on and off weight-training equipment or in getting his chair properly positioned, exercises appropriate to that equipment, and sequencing of exercises. In addition, he should learn about the components of fitness and be able to informally assess his own fitness level. Eventually, he should also be able to design his own exercise program.

• **Clear, concise, and openly communicated standards.** In John's case, his program can be kept in a binder that's accessible to all instructors at the fitness center and to John and his family.

• **Fairness in scoring procedures and their application.** John might not be receiving a grade, but the point here is related to shared understanding. If the level of achievement is predetermined together by all stakeholders in advance, then John's performance is not determined by the subjective view of an instructor. He should know his current level of achievement based on his performance, and he should have repeated opportunities to demonstrate mastery.

Given that you have the support of your supervisor, student teacher, or student coach, you should engage your participants in the design of assessment. Your role might be altered so that you work in concert with the learner. The role of arbitrator of appropriate performance standards is replaced by one of facilitating achievement. There's a greater sense of partnership in trying to achieve the goals of the program together. In other words, you can adjust instructional episodes to focus on areas that need to be achieved before the participant can reach mastery, and this will be a transparent process. The learner understands why this adjustment has taken place because he or she has participated in determining which skills need mastery. Authentic assessment becomes intertwined in instruction and is not an isolated event (Lund, 1997).

Types of Authentic Assessment

Authentic assessment types include rubrics, written work, interviews, exhibitions, portfolios, and other sources of information about what the learner knows or can do. The choice regarding the type of information to use depends on your purpose in working with the learner, the system in which your practicum is taking place, and your goals in the practicum.

Rubrics

Recording data for authentic assessment frequently involves using a rubric. A rubric specifies mutually agreed-on performance expectations and identifies levels of performance (see table 7.1). Using a rubric in conjunction with observation provides the observer with a way to focus on performance issues and remain consistent in the way assessment takes place. A rubric allows the performer knowledge of outcomes and the levels of expected achievement. Stiehl and Bessey (1993) cite seven steps to performance success:

1. The performer understands the performance task and expectations. He or she can define what the performance task is, can envision what a "good" performance looks like, and can see the link between the task and the goals.
2. The performer believes he or she will be able to perform successfully.
3. The performer recognizes the value of the task and commits to it.
4. The performer acquires the knowledge, skills, and attitudes needed to perform successfully.
5. The performer practices skills and adjusts according to feedback.
6. The performer demonstrates mastery of the task.
7. The performer claims mastery.

Designing a Rubric

Rubrics require a clear identification of the task and its components. Next, levels of competency for the components are clarified. These are then put into operation by linking them to observable behaviors. Finally, rubrics can quantify (e.g., by using a Likert-type scale) how closely the observed performance matches its descriptor. Rubrics

Table 7.1

Sample Rubric for Authentic Assessment in Floor Hockey

Simple ⟵——————————————————————————⟶ Complex

Environment	Skill development, drills, lead-up games	In–class games	School intramural games	Community Special Olympics
Skill performance	Moves to face-off with prompts and assistance	Moves to face-off without prompts	Moves quickly to face-off without prompts	Moves independently to face-off
	Passes, carries with prompts and assistance	Carries and passes without prompts	With prompts, keeps head up; passes and moves quickly during carry	Carries with head up and passes independently to the appropriate teammate
Game performance	Positions body appropriately	Carries and passes with good direction during game	Responds quickly to referee calls	Moves to position independently
	Carries around defense and passes toward goal	Moves toward the ring when receiving pass	Responds quickly to prompts to move into position	Communicates position and strategy to teammates

Frequency: Always = 3   Sometimes = 2   Never = 1

are usually designed by the instructor, but participants and other stakeholders can also participate in the process.

Using a Rubric to Understand a Person

When developed well, a rubric can illustrate an individual's strengths and weaknesses in performance. These strengths and weaknesses can then be used to establish clear goals and objectives that can be further used for program development and the organization of instruction. To accurately assess a performance, data must be gathered from a variety of sources including the learner, his or her peers, the teacher, significant others, and coaches. Data should be collected within the natural context of performance.

Actions taken on the results of the authentic assessment might include corrective feedback regarding components of the task, modifying the social and physical environment, incorporating the learner's strengths into the program, and establishing specific skills and abilities.

An advantage of the rubric is that it's designed before the program begins, so everyone in the program, including participants, knows in advance the criteria for performance at different levels. The rubric can be customized for one individual or be developed for a group. With this information, it's easy for learners to be critical of their own performance and, more important, they can focus on what they hope to achieve. By having a clear picture of where they're going, they can be more effective in creating their own achievement objectives within the program.

Written Work

Students might prefer to express their acquired knowledge in alternative ways—for example by keeping a journal on their participation in a program. Other examples include writing an essay about their health in relation to their activity program, writing about an issue within their program, or creating a short article for the school paper. Written work might also include poetry, stories, pamphlets, reviews of fitness-related Web sites, and participation guides. In community programs, this type of assessment might be recommended for wrap-up activities that accompany the final session of a program. In this type of environment, participants often focus on expressing their appreciation for instructors or leaders in addition to putting in writing what they've learned. For instructors and leaders, looking at written assessments is a good opportunity to compare their perspective of the achievements with the participants' self-assessments.

Interviews

Interviews can be highly effective for participants who use primarily verbal communication. They are also a great way to include parents, family members, and significant others. Possibilities for topics or subjects of discussion should be agreed on prior to the interview. Issues such as the length and location of the interview, whether it should be videotaped, and who will be there to watch should also be taken care of in advance. Providing the interviewee with sample questions beforehand helps reduce anxiety associated with anticipating an interview, regardless of whether it's formal or informal.

Exhibitions

If you're working with a class in your practicum, another successful alternative for authentic assessments is creating events in which achievements can be displayed in a

An exhibition is an alternative form of authentic assessment in which your class can showcase newly learned skills in a public forum.

public forum. You might schedule an exhibition or performance that showcases newly learned skills. Or you could hold a tournament or an open house. Depending on the type of program, you might consider choosing an off-site venue, such as a seniors' center, for your event.

Portfolios

Portfolios are created by accumulating materials that reflect a participant's experience in a program. The material can come from several sources, including pictures, notes from other stakeholders, videotapes, and log books. Information might also be included that's not about the participant but that's related to the program, such as pamphlets, guides, newspaper or magazine articles, and Web site information. Participants should be allowed to include whatever they feel best represents their achievements in the program. Sometimes it's appropriate to set a predetermined limit on the number of items a learner can contribute to the portfolio.

Authentic assessment suggests that individuals are assessed across a number of performances, broadening the opportunity to demonstrate competence. Because the assessment is embedded into instructional time or activity, it provides the learner more opportunities to learn and practice. And because the assessment is directly related to real tasks, it requires less transfer of learning. Finally, authentic assessment creates an opportunity for self-reflection that in turn might increase self-awareness and self-efficacy.

Concerns

Given that there are many advantages to using authentic assessment in APA, this form of assessment is gaining broad acceptance. There are concerns, however, which Lund (1997) has identified. The validity of authentic assessments can be challenged because they don't have the same level of objectivity of traditional or standardized measures. A highly detailed, specific rubric can improve the test–retest reliability of an authentic assessment, but the creativity of the design might be lost in the process. Formal assessment tools are adopted after the validity and reliability of the test have been established. Authentic assessments don't have the same types of validity and reliability checks.

When you review the literature on authentic assessment, you'll discover that there's some confusion over the terminology. The terms "authentic assessment" and "performance assessment" are often used interchangeably, much to the perplexity of kinesiologists and physical educators. For example, "A skill test would be an assessment of performance but not a performance assessment because it fails two important tests: the performance is not meaningful in and of itself, nor is it complex" (Lund, 1997, p. 28). The distinction here is that an assessment of performance indicates ability in an isolated skill, whereas a performance assessment examines the ability to use that skill in a game situation or activity in which the skill is part of a larger performance of ability.

Rubrics are not easy to write well, and they should be done well in advance of offering a program. This can make the task more difficult because a rubric should include several factors that might be difficult to determine accurately before a participant starts his or her program. To create a rubric properly takes a lot of time. Keep in mind that several stakeholders (participant, parents, classroom teacher) might want to contribute to the process. Other considerations include the number of participants that require assessment, who will be receiving the assessments, and, most important, the purpose of doing an assessment.

Compatibility Overlap

The choice of assessments depends on many factors, including the requirements of the agency where you're placed, the reason for the assessment, and your beliefs about motor development. Be sure to ask your supervisor if the agency or school has a preferred method of assessment. If so, learn the method and use it.

You might be undertaking an assessment for many reasons. Perhaps you need to know your learners' current skills and ability level so that you can adequately plan a program. Or you might be joining an existing program and want to determine how far an individual has progressed. Or you might be at the end of your practicum and want to measure your success in working with the person. Regardless, your assessment tool must be consistent with the goals of the program.

Finally, your beliefs about motor development might influence your choice of assessment method. If you believe that development is hierarchical and orderly, then a standardized assessment that addresses the pieces of motor development and takes into account the age and developmental stage of the individual fits your belief system. If you believe that a systems model better describes motor development, then you'll want to use an assessment that takes into account multiple sources of data collected in several environments under differing conditions. Assessing this way is more congruent with informal and authentic assessments.

Authentic assessments and formal assessments are based on differing belief systems about what's most important. Formal assessments are based on normative theory and base results on how closely performance matches a typical or normal performance. They are congruent with views of disability related to deviance. Comparing to a norm suggests that we're trying to make a person with a disability fall into the norm.

Authentic assessments relate to a person's real-life experiences and anticipate variability. They are more congruent with a socially constructed view of disability. In adapted physical activity there's a strong case for authentic assessment because it's individual centered and relative to a person's functional boundaries.

Assessing Environmental Support Systems

Successful participation in a program depends on the psychological, social, and physical aspects of the environment. Negative and stereotypical attitudes restrict full involvement of people with disabilities. This type of attitude can stem from lack of knowledge, a nonworkable situation, or awkward or negative experiences. Factors that can improve attitudes include providing an orientation to everyone who takes part in the program. Often managers or instructors will provide an orientation for teacher aids or volunteers, but they overlook providing a similar orientation to all the participants in a program. Nondisabled participants might be hesitant to get involved with people with disability for fear of unintentionally harming them or insulting them because they've offered help when none is needed. These apprehensions can be dispelled through an orientation that includes a participant with a disability. Another technique that might be used is simulation exercises, which can change attitudes and reduce misunderstanding through increased awareness. If done inappropriately, feelings of pity might result, which is the opposite of what's desired. Empathy is not pity but a feeling of being one with others. Empathy doesn't suggest that people without disability can understand what it's like to have a disability. But it does suggest that they can understand, for instance, what it's like to have to turn a wheelchair around in an elevator in order to reach the buttons.

Research on simulation in APA (Emes & Legg, 2004) found mixed feelings among people with disability about using simulations in APA. Some people with disability don't support simulations under any conditions. Olkin (1999) offers the following reasons not to use simulations:

- They don't simulate disability.
- Simulating a disability for a short period of time can't approach the psychological impact of "forever."
- Simulation doesn't address disability as a social construct.
- Simulation doesn't reflect a minority model of disability in which the locus of impairment resides in society.
- There's no quantitative evidence that simulation exercises work.
- Students might think they understand disability after simulation and abandon further study of disability.

- There are ethical issues to consider. For example, is it offensive and rude to attempt to imitate a person with a disability?

Other people with disability believe simulations are useful if several criteria are met. Kiger (1992) supports simulation only with several caveats. These include clarifying the theoretical connection between the simulation and changing attitude, careful design of the exercise, assessing the risks and benefits to the participants, and post-simulation evaluation.

If there's support for it at your practicum site, simulation can be a useful tool for assessing the environment. From a standing position, all the items listed in exercise 7.2 later in this chapter might appear to adequately accommodate everyone. With your sight, everything might appear to be well positioned on the floor plan. But if you test these perceptions from a wheelchair or with a blindfold on, you might discover otherwise. Key to a supportive physical environment is providing complete access and engagement within the environment without a sense of awkwardness. Change should not stress being different; change should be good for everyone. A supportive physical environment is accessible to everyone and facilitates engagement for anyone participating in the programs. At the end of the chapter, exercise 7.3 provides a framework for you to use in conducting an environmental assessment at your practicum site.

Assessment is an ongoing process of improvement. The things you discover that require change should be corrected. Report your findings to your practicum supervisor, and try to get these items on a list of things to be changed.

Summary

Assessments can be used for many purposes, including placement decisions for students, program development, and the development of appropriate environments for learners. Some assessment tools are standardized and include specific information on data collection and evaluation. Other assessment tools involve comparing the person's performance to a list of criteria that is specific to an activity. A more recent development is the use of authentic assessments, which take into account the requirements of the activity and the natural environment in which the activity occurs. An assessment process that is comprehensive in nature and gathers data in a variety of ways is typically the most useful in determining the compatibility between the person and the activity.

Exercise 7.1
Functional Assessment Leading to a Compatibility Match

Determine the level of the compatibility match between the person and the activity that you're working with in your practicum.

TIP The relative importance of each factor varies depending on the type of activity. Determine which factors are most important, and focus on them first; then complete the remaining factor assessments accordingly. For example, object manipulation in a racket sport or ball game requires a higher functional level of object manipulation than does swimming.

	Learner's functional abilities	Functional abilities required for the activity
Mobility		
Object manipulation		
Cognitive function		
Communication and perception		
Behavior and social skills		
Fitness		

1. What is the level of compatibility?

_____

_____

2. What are the areas that require accommodation?

_____

_____

_____

3. What are this person's overall health and safety issues that must be addressed?

_____

_____

_____

Exercise 7.2
Positions of Olkin and Kiger

Review the positions of Olkin and Kiger regarding simulation of disability exercises as described earlier in this chapter.

1. What is your opinion or belief regarding the use of simulations? Why do you think this way? Is there evidence in the environment that supports your position?

_____

_____

_____

_____

_____

_____

2. Ask people with disability for their opinions on simulations. Probe their responses to find out why they have that opinion. Then share the thinking of Olkin and Kiger with them, and ask for their response. (You need not identify these people by name when you record their responses.)

_____

_____

_____

_____

Sample Assessment for the Practicum Environment

Fill in the blanks with observations you make for each area. If appropriate, use the following guide to assess the environment of the facility where your practicum takes place.

1. Psychosocial environment

    a. Attitudes: _____

    b. Orientation: _____

    c. Person-first language: _____

    d. Language with dignity: _____

2. Accessibility and physical environment

    a. Ramps: _____

    b. Elevator (height of buttons, height of emergency phone, Braille buttons, size [e.g., for turning a wheelchair around]): _____

    c. Stair railings on both sides of the stairwell: _____

    d. Nonslip surface on the stairs: _____

    e. Width of stairwell: _____

    f. Door width: _____

    g. Door opening (opens in, opens out, sliding, electric, remote opener): _____

    _____

    h. Doorknobs (round, handle, lever, other): _____

    i. Nonskid floor surface: _____

3. Lighting: _____

4. Signage Braille: _____

5. Telephone

    a. Height: _____

    b. Braille: _____

6. Washroom

    a. Doors (open in/out, handle): _____

    b. Stalls (seat heights, railing, wheelchair accessible): _____

    c. Sinks (height): _____

7. Locker rooms or changing rooms

    a. Lockers (height, wheelchair accessible): _____

    b. Showers (wheelchair accessible): _____

    c. Nonskid floor surface: _____

8. Describe other physical factors that influence the environment at the location of your practicum.

_____

_____

_____

_____

9. After your assessment, what recommendations would you forward to your supervisor?

_____

_____

_____

_____

_____

_____

_____

Exercise 7.4
Rubric

Create a rubric for a task that the person you're working with is learning during your practicum.

TIP Review the section on rubrics on pages 85-86, the seven steps to performance success, the section on designing rubrics, and the example in table 7.1. In the table, notice how the environment changes to a progressively more challenging setting. At the same time, skill and game performance demonstrate high levels of complexity.

Part III

LOOKING BACK:
Evaluation

"Education is what survives when what has been learned has been forgotten."

B.F. Skinner (1904–1990), *New Scientist,* May 21, 1964

8

Reviewing Your Competencies

"The self is not something ready-made, but something in continuous formation through choice of action."

John Dewey (1859–1952)

Jennifer is nearing the end of her practicum. She can't believe it's almost over. Her last journal entry says, "Wow, today was the best day ever. When I look around, I feel like I belong here. Erin has really gotten the hang of the floor program, and today she even used some of the gymnastics equipment. Her mom was waiting for me when I arrived with a gift to thank me for all I have done. The staff at the Boys and Girls Club want me to come back and work for them. But I'm not sure if I should. If I come back to the same place and same program, will I continue to learn? Am I so comfortable here that I function without reflecting on what I am doing? Plus, I really feel that I have a better understanding of children with cerebral palsy within an inclusive program. Now I am ready to work with people who have other challenges in performance. I wonder what my APA instructor thinks about me. She only came to see me once, so I guess she is relying on what the staff here says. I know I shouldn't care about my grade, but it's important if I want to go to grad school."

Throughout your practicum you've used reflection as a way to identify your own strengths and needs. You've done this formally through the exercises in this book and informally through discussions with others and reflective writing in your journal. Together, these activities help you better understand your practicum experience. Now it's time to try to make sense of your learning.

Reviewing What You Know

Review what you have recorded in your journal and through the exercises you have completed. If you were going to summarize what you know, what would you say? As you formulate a response, remember that you're knowledgeable about many things. For example, what do you know about your personal traits as revealed through the practicum? Are you a patient person? Do you have high expectations of yourself and others? What do you know about health impairments? What do you know about people with disability? What do you know about the organization to which you provided services? What do you know about the physical and social environments in which your service occurred?

Reviewing What You Did

Next, review the chronological elements of your journal. How long did your practicum last? What roles and responsibilities did you fill during your practicum? You might have provided service to a group or to one person. Was this what you expected? What happened that was unexpected? When you compare what you know about yourself to what you did in the practicum, were you comfortable working with people with disability? What influenced those feelings? If you expected a hands-on experience, did the practicum meet your expectations? How so or why not? Can you name times when you were particularly successful or not successful? What influenced your interpretation of success? Figure 8.1 illustrates how what you know and what you did contribute to learning and learning outcomes.

Reviewing Your Results

To appreciate the learning you experienced during your practicum, you need to integrate information from what you know and what you did. One way to do this is to compare and contrast the outcomes in each area and then write a summary. A second way is to construct a graphic organizer or concept map that shows your results. Another way to visualize the same integration of ideas is presented in figure 8.2 (page 102).

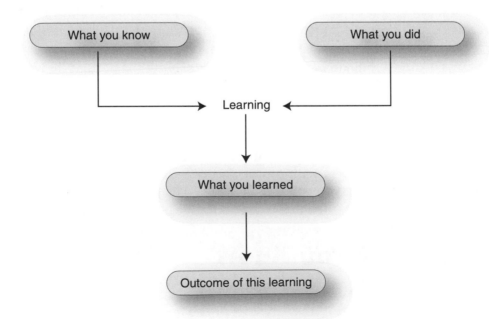

Figure 8.1 Knowing about yourself.

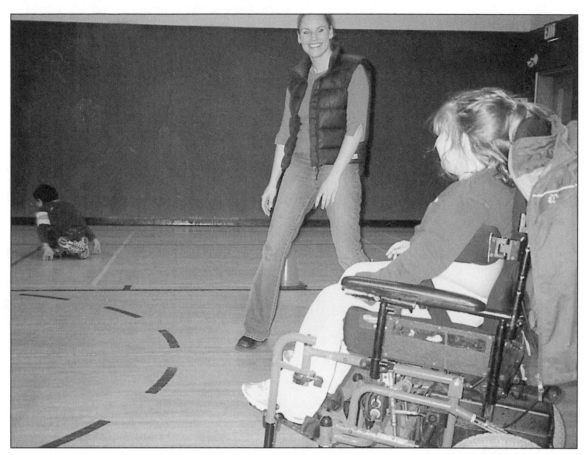

When reviewing what you did in your practicum, you must ask yourself many questions. For example, what roles did you fill? Were your experiences expected? Were you comfortable?

Reviewing What Others Know About You

When you think about it, you realize that there are things only you know about yourself, things that both you and others know, and things that others know about you that you might not know yet. A practicum is a unique experience because you're receiving feedback from many sources. Your supervisor shares his or her knowledge of your skills and abilities relative to your agency responsibilities. Your instructor gives you information on how well you're able to use your course knowledge in the real world. And the person with whom you're working lets you know how well you're able to interact and communicate with people with disability. This negotiation of knowledge that occurs among you and others is the social construction of knowledge. Figure 8.3 demonstrates this point with a holistic view of learning. Sometimes what you think you know and what others tell you is contradictory. The best thing to do when this occurs is to take time to understand the differences in viewpoints. To do this, try to listen without making an immediate judgment. A technique to give yourself time is to summarize what the other person told you and then ask if he or she agrees that your summary is accurate. Another easy trick is to take a deep breath and count to five. What is important is that you actively listen to and absorb the feedback you're receiving.

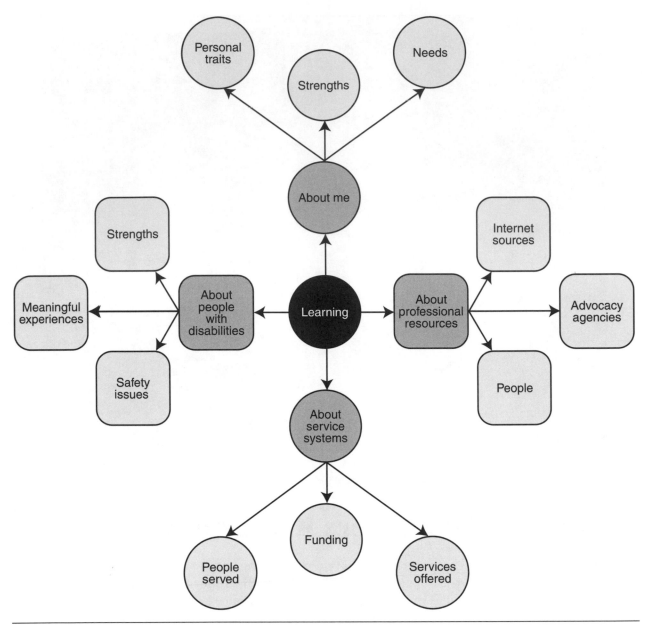

Figure 8.2 Understanding personal competencies in relation to the practicum.

Preparing to Deal With Constructive Feedback

Before you can understand feedback and use it in a constructive way, you need to identify your "hot spots." A hot spot represents a part of ourselves that causes us to respond negatively when it is "pushed" by another person or event. Sometimes a hot spot is centered on the nonverbal body language of the other person. Constructive feedback about something you believed you had done well might also create a hot spot. Often, feedback regarding our values and beliefs creates discomfort.

What about positive and constructive feedback? Many of us have trouble accepting a compliment. It's important to you and the person giving you the compliment that you acknowledge it and accept it. Don't question the integrity of the message by countering it with your own negative statements!

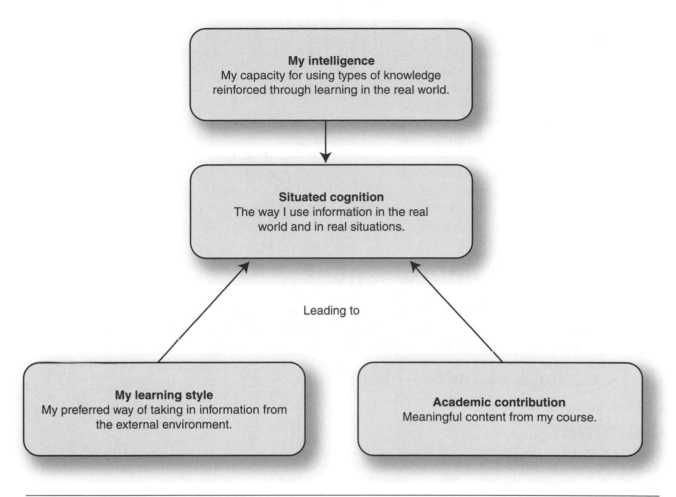

Figure 8.3 Holistic view of learning.

This practicum is one part of a myriad of learning activities that you're experiencing simultaneously. To make the best use of the practicum, remember that learning is a relatively permanent change in behavior. This means that the outcomes of this practicum experience need to be congruent with your educational and career goals. The feedback you receive from your course instructor and agency supervisor is part of their responsibility and is meant to help you become a better professional.

Reviewing Postevaluation Outcomes

Evaluation is the process of reviewing what you know and determining the relative value in comparison to your goals. This requires critical thinking. During examination of your knowledge, it's important to ask, How do I know this? How do I feel about this knowledge? Try to be objective. Can you examine what you know from another person's perspective? Can you relinquish your viewpoint in favor of one that might facilitate more growth? Can you distinguish between fact and opinion? This process might require you to tolerate discomfort, anxiety, and conflict. Good, helpful evaluation takes time.

To use the information you have gathered and synthesized about your learning, you need to communicate the outcomes and your intent to others. When doing so, try to use "I"-based messages. The content of these messages might include your observations, feelings, thoughts, needs, and intentions. For example, "I was able to use the assessments in the practicum to choose activities that Toni, my learner, could do. I felt successful because I made appropriate choices. I believe this occurred because of the information presented in my course. I want to know more about how to provide appropriate resources so that Toni can continue with these activities. I intend to contact the Disabled Skiing Association to ask if there are supports available so that Toni can join the organization and continue skiing."

Learning from feedback requires you to determine who "owns" the information and any problems identified. The next step requires you to employ active listening skills that include reflection, restatement, and clarification. During this process, you'll be determining the congruence between what's being said, the body language of the speaker, and the message being sent. Finally, you need to compare the feedback to your goals. If you think that responding to the feedback by making some changes will help you achieve your goals, develop an action plan to help you to act on the feedback.

Learning for Improvement

Now it's time to go back to the learning plan you constructed in chapter 4. Identify the objectives that you met or partially met. Identify what helped you to meet these objectives. Next, address the objectives you didn't meet. Highlight them. Brainstorm what you can do to meet them. Choose one or two ideas that you believe are realistic and develop an action plan for meeting the objectives. Implement your plan.

Summary

Understanding what you learned in your practicum helps you to determine your level of competency in adapted physical activity. This chapter helped you to review what you did and what you know based on information from others and yourself, and provided some suggestions on dealing with feedback. Your practicum was implemented to help you apply material from your course and to give you an opportunity to learn through experience. After completing the exercises at the end of this chapter, you should have a good sense of the outcomes of your experiences.

The exercises that follow are meant to help you understand the learning experience provided in your practicum. Choose one of the exercises to complete. Based on the results identified through these exercises, write a paragraph that summarizes your practicum.

Exercise 8.1
Reviewing Competencies

Choose one of the following formats to present the results of your analysis of what you know and what you did:

1. Fill in the chart in the following table, *What you know about yourself* and *Roles you filled*, to perform your assessment of what you learned through the roles you played.

TIP Reread the sections on reviewing what you know and what you did, and look in your journal for examples of your competencies.

Table 8.1

Reviewing Competencies

	What you know about yourself	What you know about health impairments	What you know about people with disability	What you know about service systems
Roles you filled	(e.g., evaluator)	(e.g., learner)	(e.g., friend)	(e.g., student instructor or assistant)
Responsibilities you completed	(e.g., self-assessment)	(e.g., assigned reading from text)	(e.g., established a professional relationship with participants)	(e.g., learned safety policies)
Tasks you did	(e.g., journaling weekly)	(e.g., environmental safety assessment)	(e.g., advocated for better time for program)	(e.g., made sure facility was properly set up before participants arrived)

or

2. Collage: Use several different materials to create a collage that depicts you as you have come to understand yourself through this practicum. Ideas for materials include colored tissue paper, magazine pictures, found objects, paint or markers, and natural objects. The materials can be mounted, if you wish, to create a two- or three-dimensional collage or montage. The finished product should include true representations of your physical being along with symbols (pictures, words, color) of what you value and believe in. For example, Erin's collage included photos of her practicum site, words that represented what she learned, and a small mirror that symbolized the reflectiveness she developed through her journaling. Share this product with your course instructor or agency supervisor.

Reviewing Practicum and Career Goals

Relate your practicum to your career goals by completing this questionnaire.

TIP The first statement in the exercise is about learning. Learning takes on many different forms; you might think of learning in terms of gaining new information, but learning might also involve the way you approach things or the way you interact with others. For example, the following journal entry reflects a change in the way this person thinks: *I am really finding myself seeing Tom's abilities versus disabilities. Instead of asking myself, "Is Tom going to be able to complete this activity?" I ask, "What can Tom do?" I suppose this indicates a possible change in my thinking, an important step toward my taking an abilities-based approach to things.* (5 weeks into practicum)

Complete the following statements:

One thing I learned was_____

One question I still have is _____

One thing I found interesting is _____

One application for this is _____

I still need help with _____

Complete the following statements:

When I think of someone who has a disability, I feel _____

When I think of someone who has a disability, I see_____

When I think of someone with a disability, I know_____

Recall a time in your practicum when you encountered a problem. Describe the problem and how you resolved it.

_____

_____

_____

_____

_____

_____

9

Program Evaluation

"The person who makes a success of living is the one who sees his goal steadily and aims for it unswervingly. That is dedication."

Cecil B. DeMille (1881–1959)

Frank has been involved in an after-school sports program as part of his practicum. From the beginning, his instructor made it clear that she wanted to know how Frank felt about the program and if the program related to the APA course he was taking. Frank's instructor told him that this was the first time a student had been placed in this practicum, and she wanted to know from the student's perspective if it was a good placement. Frank worried about placing that value judgment on the program; after all, if he said it was not good, did that mean the program would have to do without a student staff member in the future? Frank felt strongly that the program needed more hands; at times he felt the program strayed from its goal of participation for every child. Now the staff person from the program was asking for his input in terms of the progress of the three children Frank had worked with. Should he be honest with her? What if the lack of improvement documented for Patrick meant Patrick wouldn't be a part of the program in the future? Finally, Frank's course instructor told him she expected Frank to share his evaluation of the agency program relative to the APA course and Frank's learning. He wondered if this evaluation would affect his grade.

Evaluation involves the systematic collection of data for several purposes. Evaluation can provide information about activities and outcomes that reveal what programs are actually doing and affecting, relative to the intentions that were the basis of the program design. This information can be used to assist decision making, assess the overall need for the program, determine if some parts of a program are not working, determine how participants view the program, and document how well the program is working. The most important reason to evaluate is to improve the program.

In an APA practicum, program evaluation is used by the agency, your instructor and you, and the student to determine if the program has been successful. By its very nature, program evaluation requires gathering data from several sources. For example, you might give the agency information about how the participants performed, if the participants were satisfied with the program, what activities appeared to be the most useful, and what difficulties you perceived in the program. You might provide your instructor with information about how well the program met the course requirements, what changes you suggest to improve the APA practicum, and what you learned in the practicum that related to the course content. Your role in the program evaluation process needs to be identified before you begin the APA practicum. Doing so will help you in recording information throughout your practicum and in determining what assessments you'll use in your practicum. If you'll be part of the evaluation process used by the agency, then the data you provide must be in a form that's usable by the agency. The data must relate to the program goals and objectives. If you're part of the program evaluation process your instructor uses to determine how the agency program will be used for future APA practica, then your data must relate to the goals and objectives of the course and the practicum itself. You also need to determine how you felt about the program. Although this is a less formal procedure, it's related to the assessment of your own learning you completed in chapter 8.

When you provide this data to the agency or your instructor at the end of your experience, it's part of a summative evaluation process. Sometimes you're asked to provide ongoing information, as part of a formative evaluation process, in which the feedback you provide can be used to make changes in the program so it has a better chance of success.

In this chapter we'll discuss types of program evaluation, types of data used in program evaluation, and sources of this data. Your role in the program evaluation process depends on your instructor and the agency for which you're completing the APA practicum. Finally, the chapter will discuss alternative views of disability. Why is this important? If an APA practicum and the programs it uses view disability as residing in the individual, then specific evaluation data types and sources are chosen. For example, some people view disability as the individual's problem and focus on "fixing" the person. They disregard the environments in which the individual resides. If the practicum and program views disability as being defined by the society in which we all live, then the data types and data sources used must be congruent with this view of disability. You need to know about both views, understand each one, and reflect on your own view because it will influence your decisions about program evaluation.

Assumptions About Evaluation

Evaluation is useful when it's based on quality information. Generally, a program evaluation is unique to the program that's being reviewed , so the scheme for evaluation should be responsible yet flexible. Hellison, Cutforth, Kallusky, Martinek, Parker, and Stiehl (2000) identified assumptions that have guided their evaluation efforts in a youth program. Four of their assumptions resonate with programming in adapted physical activity. We have added a fifth from our own experiences.

1. **Commit to making a difference.** The purpose and motive for evaluating might vary among programs, but accountability is a common reason to evaluate. Accountability relates to how money is spent, how well the program met the agency goals, how well the program matched its agency's philosophy or mission, and whether the program made a difference. Ultimately, the evaluation should help the program in making a positive difference—one that translates into making a difference for the participants. This reinforces the reason for collecting data from the participants during the process.

2. **There's no one best way to evaluate.** Because of the many considerations and variables that must be taken into account with each program, there can be no one best method or design for program evaluation. Some of these considerations include the physical environment, the community, and the abilities of the participants. Partici-

pant abilities show broad variability, thus each program is unique and will benefit from a design customized for that program. The choices and decisions made about the evaluation design and process should be guided by the potential usefulness of the data it will generate. The evaluation device must demonstrate responsiveness to the needs and interests of the participants as well as the staff and volunteers in the program.

3. **Evaluations can be conducted by insiders.** You might think that for an evaluation to be effective it must be objective, and that the only way to ensure objectivity is to assign the task of evaluation to an outsider. Indeed, an outsider might bring objectivity to the process, but it's unlikely that he or she will bring the same understanding or meaning to the data as someone who's intimately connected to the program. Despite the scientific position that biasing might affect results because of the evaluator's closeness to the data, Hellison et al. (2000) argue that biasing is not all bad. They believe that to effectively relate the findings, staff and program participants must be involved in every aspect of the evaluation program, including development, delivery, and application.

4. **Evaluation findings are useful to all stakeholders.** As a reminder, stakeholders are those people who are affected by the program, including participants, family members, practicum students, teachers, coaches, physiotherapists, fitness instructors, volunteers, and those funding the program. In a broad sense, stakeholders also include the community at large—because we hope that APA programs truly make a difference in the lives of all community residents.

Data that will effect change must be useful to everyone who is being affected by and participates in the program. This means the information should be accurate, easy to interpret, useful, and communicated in a way that all stakeholders can understand and find meaningful.

5. **Creativity is essential.** To determine the effectiveness of a program and produce data that has a positive impact, you might have to use unusual or nontraditional ways of gathering information. There's no reason to limit methods for learning about a program. In a section later in the chapter we discuss finding the learner's voice and offer several examples of nontraditional, creative ways to evaluate. Creativity is a personal attribute that we often hide, but using your imagination to think of new ways to collect useful evaluative information is something we promote in adapted physical activity.

Types of Evaluation

Each of the several types of program evaluation serves a purpose. Although we've emphasized the need for developing and designing program-specific evaluations, the purpose of different evaluations puts them into broad categories.

Global Program Evaluation

Global program evaluation takes into account the entire program. It synthesizes information from each discrete program session and addresses areas of strength in the program itself. For example, an adapted aquatics program that focuses on swim lessons could be evaluated by determining the progression of all of its participants across the span of the program. A global program evaluation also takes into account how well facilities met the needs of the program, how effective staff and volunteers were in accomplishing program goals, and how satisfactory the materials and equipment were for staff, volunteers, and participants. Later in this chapter you'll have the opportunity to complete a global evaluation of your practicum program (exercise 9.1).

Program evaluation can be formative or summative in nature. Recall that a formative evaluation is done while the program is occurring. Its purpose is to assess the program and make relevant changes to enhance the program's ability to meet individual participant needs. A summative program evaluation is done at the end of the program. Its purpose is to determine the program's success and to account for the expenditure of staff and agency resources. Neither of these types of program evaluation can occur without addressing the achievements of the program participants.

Participant Achievement Evaluation

By reviewing the achievements of participants in a program, you're looking at the key factors associated with measuring the effectiveness of a program. Individual program participants have their own goals for participation. Usually, these occur parallel to goals set by the agency or institution; family or significant others might also have goals for the learner. Evaluation of achievements might take into account all three perspectives. Not every student involved in a practicum will be asked by his or her agency supervisor or academic instructor to evaluate based on all three perspectives. You need to clarify the expectations of those to whom you are accountable. But you should take the time to conduct an evaluation of achievements that will be part of your journal, both as an exercise in evaluating program effectiveness and as a culminating contribution to your record of participation in the practicum. This task might feel somewhat familiar because in chapters 1 and 8 you completed a different part of the evaluation process—a self-evaluation. As a practicum student, you have goals that you developed relative to your placement. Your goals existed alongside goals set by your academic instructor

An integral part in determining the effectiveness of a program is to review the achievements of the participants.

and agency supervisor. You completed your self-evaluation in this context. So, you're like a program participant in this area! Keep your own evaluation in mind as we now examine the evaluation process relative to program participants.

In chapter 7 we discussed the use of authentic assessments and standardized assessments, reviewing how each might be used in your practicum. Evaluating the progress of your program participants depends on the decisions you made about the assessment process. If you're using standardized assessments, an efficient way to determine if progress has occurred is to administer pre- and post-tests. At the beginning of your practicum, administer the standardized assessment and at the end, repeat the assessment. The difference in scores is one way to measure changes and achievement. Keep in mind that a standardized assessment doesn't take into account whole activities or the effects of a natural environment. It will be difficult for you to determine if the participant's achievements are generalized into his or her typical lifestyle. Remember that standardized tests address the issue of normal performance and are based on a deviance model. Part of what the test is meant to do is indicate whether the participant's performance is now closer to that of his or her typical peers.

Authentic assessments involve continual review of a person's achievements. Because these assessments take place in natural environments, they might be more effective in helping you determine how the learner incorporates learning into his or her lifestyle. Authentic assessments take into account participant's goals and those of his or her significant others related to factors other than performance measures. To accomplish this assessment we must introduce the learner's voice into the assessment.

Listening to the Learner's Voice

First of all, who is the learner? In a practicum situation, the learner is both you and the program participants with whom you're working. What is the learner's voice? It is that piece of ourselves that we know about and choose to share with others; it exists alongside knowledge about ourselves that others know but that we fail to see. It's important to understand that each of us also has insights about ourselves and our performance that we don't share with others; plus, we each have developing knowledge about ourselves that is not yet in our consciousness. Being open to the learner's voice begins with acknowledging your own assumptions and stereotypes. Our values and attitudes about others who are different are strong determinants in our beliefs about their abilities.

How Do You Recognize the Learner's Voice?

Each person has a unique style of communicating with others. For example, some people share information best through speech. Others use alternative methods, such as sign language or assisted communication technology. A person's body language—his or her expressions of meaning through facial expressions and gestures—are significant in the communication process. In the motor arena, a person's physical performance is a method of communication. Body position, tone, and fluidity of movement all have meaning. This type of communication occurs both in physical activity and in drama. Written language in the form of stories, personal narratives, and poetry provide another way of sharing information. Finally, music plays a role in sharing our voice with others. Note that these methods of communication are consistent with the concept of multiple intelligences discussed in chapter 6.

Body language is a significant part of the communication process.

How Do You Access the Learner's Voice?

You access the learner's voice through your conscious choice of activities and evaluations that are diverse and creative. For example, in a student practicum with a disabled skiing organization, data-collection tools might include poetry written by the learner that focuses on the learner's affective changes as his or her skiing competence increases. This data could be coupled with criteria-based assessment that addresses specific physical skills and abilities. A knowledge-based test of the equipment needed for skiing and the safety rules to be followed would provide important information on the cognitive domain. Finally, because skiing involves rhythm, the learner might compose a song using percussion instruments that illustrates the tempo of weight shifts and ski transitions. Deciding when and how to use these diverse and creative methods of data collection depends on whether your evaluation plan is formative or summative. In a formative evaluation process, you might stagger each type of data collection method across the length of the program. Then you would use the data analysis to make appropriate changes to the program while it is operating. For a summative evaluation, you would use the data analysis to evaluate the entire program and recommend changes to be instituted the next time it is offered.

Developing a Constructive Review

Your view of disability is influenced by what you believe regarding the way our world functions. Using the concept of a continuum, you might see disability as a problem that rests entirely with the person who has the disability. The person is disabled because he or she is different in physical capacity, intellectual capacity, or psychological ability from the majority of people in the society. If we could just "fix" the person, then he or she would be more like the majority and thus less disabled. How do we "fix" the person? Often our attempted "fixes" are through medical treatments such as pharmaceutical agents, interventions such as strengthening programs, or behavior management programs based on psychological principles. An alternative view to the one just described is that disability is constructed by a society—a group of people. The disability can be "deconstructed" by providing supports, changing attitudes and belief systems, and opening services on an equal basis to all members of the society. For example, providing physical environments that allow access to everyone including those who use wheelchairs, those who are visually impaired, and those with endurance problems creates a context that eliminates differences among people, thereby reducing disability.

Understanding the Context

In abilities-based adapted physical activity we view a person in terms of his or her capacities. In chapter 1 we urged you to see the *person* first, not his or her disability. Disability is a consideration only when it prevents a person from achieving his or her goals. Unfortunately, one perspective of disability that persists is the idea of deviance. In other words, someone is disabled when he or she is different from the "typical" member of a population. We generally use parameters for these judgments based on developmental domains, such as the motor or physical domain, cognitive domain, and psychological or affective domain. Thus we label people as physically handicapped, deaf, mentally ill, or mentally handicapped. Such labeling frequently leads to special and segregated services in which the domain itself becomes the predominant area for change. For example, people who have an intellectual disability go to a special classroom in which instruction is different, they perform segregated physical activities in which the rules are different, and they participate in sheltered social situations for the protection. The problems and solutions lie within the person with the disability, and if he or she is helped to more closely approximate "normal," he or she will have a better life.

This view of disablement as deviance comes from a variety of sources, including the visual media, newspaper and magazines, advertisements, movies, peers, and our own significant others. In some cases we acquire this view of disability because of the absence of people with disability. For example, until recently, few people with disability appeared in advertisements or as television actors. More recently, advertisements do include people in wheelchairs, and there are TV and film roles for and about people with disability. Print media conveys attitudes and values through language choice. Frequently terms such as "confined to a wheelchair" or "afflicted with cerebral palsy" and "the disabled" are used with little conscious regard for the negative impact they have on the reader.

We also make judgments about people with disability based on the point in life at which the impairment was acquired. Working with young children who have a congenital condition, such as cerebral palsy or Down syndrome, might elicit more pity than empathy. The visibility of the impairment makes a difference in the reactions of others. The more different someone looks, the more difficult it is to accept the person as normal. This appears to be especially true with people who have facial disfigurements.

Finally, how comprehensible the disability is to others is critical in forming one's disablement view. Knowledge of etiology, pathophysiology, signs and symptoms, and medical management can either increase or decrease the apprehension of others without the disability. This type of thinking that focuses on the medical condition supports the continuation of exclusion in our society, yet our thinking and concerns about disability in society went on for years "without disabled people, leading disabled theorists such as James Charlton . . . to proclaim 'Nothing about us without us'" (Michalko, 2002, p. 167).

A relatively new perspective that disability is socially constructed has emerged. As a social construction, disability must be dealt with in the existing social reality in which the individual exists. In contrast to the positivist or deviance view, a socially constructed view of disability focuses on the idea that the environment itself defines who is disabled and who is not. In this case, "environment" is considered from its broadest perspective and includes the physical environment (manmade and natural), temporal environment, social environment, cultural environment, and political environment.

For example, in the political environment, the Americans With Disabilities Act—a law in the United States—specifically defines disabilities and lists the health conditions and impairments included. Learning disabilities are a part of this law. Yet a person with a learning disability might not be perceived as disabled in many social situations.

The World Health Organization (WHO) assumed a similar perspective in 2001 with the official launch of the International Classification of Functioning, Disability, and Health (ICF). ICF changes our understanding of disability from a medical problem orientation to a person perspective. By adopting this perspective, the organization now focuses on how measures can be targeted to optimize a person's ability. WHO has further expanded their perspective to include two contextual factors that influence disability and functioning: environmental and personal factors. The ICF takes into account the social aspects of disability and provides a mechanism to document the impact of the social and physical environment on a person's functioning.

As part of the understanding of disability as a social construct, terminology is a critical concern. According to Lonsdale (1990), two schools of thought exist. One school argues that the use of the term "disabled" serves as a blanket term, referring to a large number of people who have nothing in common except "that they do not function in exactly the same way as people who are called 'normal' or 'able-bodied'" (p. 2). Others use the term to define a social minority, accepting the possibility that discrimination might occur as a result.

> In this context, it is seen to encourage feelings of solidarity, strength and supportiveness among a group of people whose disparate physical characteristics are uniformly used to oppress them—rather like the slogan "black is beautiful" was used to turn around a negative concept in the 1960s. (Lonsdale, 1990, p. 2)

Partially in response to the concern about terminology, many voluntary associations have changed their names. In Canada, for example, most organizations no longer use the name "Association for the Mentally Retarded" in their titles. Most leave out the term "mentally retarded" altogether (Johnson, 1985). More recently, associations are using the label "associations for community living" (Brown, 1992). This is an attempt to reduce the implication that all people with an intellectual disability are the same.

Writing the Constructive Review

In developing a constructive review of a participant's performance that will contribute to the data used in program evaluation, you must make many decisions. What will you call the participant? From a socially constructed view of disability, you would probably call him or her by name or by a pseudonym to protect his or her confidentiality and privacy. Other terms that might be used include third-person references—the learner, the participant, the athlete, and the like. The focus on the language is the important piece of the writing. In chapter 1, we discussed the importance of language with dignity—for example, less acceptable terms would be "the patient," "the disabled or handicapped person," or the "cp student." If you need to use an impairment label, use person-first terminology—the student with cerebral palsy.

A second issue to address is how to express change. Do you reflect progress or lack of it by comparing a person with a disability to a typical person? If so, what words do you choose? Do you believe there's such a thing as a "normal" person? Do you talk about both positive progress and areas of weakness? Is movement toward independence an issue? Do you reflect on supports and barriers in the environment? Your answers to these questions relate to your perspective on disability. If you see disablement as deviance, your report will include statements about the medical condition, a comparison of the person's performance to a typical person relative to the established goals and assessments, statements about areas of need, and recommendations about future programs or activities that might help change the person.

Our concept of disability shapes how we represent disability and evaluate people with disability. If you believe in disability as a social construction, your report will begin with a description of the learner that identifies strengths and weaknesses relative to the goals developed for the learner in the program. You'll also describe strengths and weaknesses related to the learner's own goals and those of significant others. Your report will relate this information to the person's lifestyle. Following this, your report will identify how each type of environment limits or enhances performance. Your recommendations will identify programs and activities that help the learner progress toward the established goals and changes that need to occur in each type of environment.

The organization of the report, regardless of your view of disablement, will follow the format determined by your agency supervisor and academic instructor. There are times when this becomes a problem. If you believe in disability as a social construct, but the agency you're working for and your academic supervisor require a report that includes a focus on medical issues and a checklist of behaviors, this lack of congruence between beliefs and reporting style is critical. If this occurs, you need to find a way to discuss the issue with your instructor and supervisor. A similar problem occurs if you believe in disablement as deviance, and your reporting form asks you for a narrative report that focuses on context.

Collecting Information or Data

Evaluation can't be conducted without collecting information or data about the participants and other components of the program, how the program is delivered, and the effect the program has on the participants and other people associated with them or the program. To be useful, information consistent with the goals of the program should be collected according to a plan that specifies a time frame for collecting different types of information and a schedule that includes all the appropriate contributors. The most important consideration is to identify processes and outcomes useful to those involved in the program.

Methods of collecting data will vary according to the information being sought and the source of the information. Generally, you'll compile data using questionnaires, surveys, observations, interviews, journals, and perhaps other methods.

Questionnaire or Survey

A questionnaire can be designed that's unique to the program and also has a potential for repeated use. It can be used as both a formative and summative tool. It can also be used from year to year with appropriate modifications that reflect program changes based on the information gathered from evaluations done the previous year. Questionnaires are relatively straightforward to construct and administer. The data can be quantitative, qualitative, or a combination. Questionnaires can be completed verbally or in written form and by a proxy, if necessary. At the end of this chapter a sample program questionnaire provides quantitative data, using a Likert scale to measure respondent agreement with program assessment, and qualitative data generated from comment boxes (exercise 9.1). An appropriate questionnaire for your program can be created from this sample.

Observations

Watching and recording what you see can be an effective way of generating useful data for evaluating programs. In chapter 2 you learned about making good observational statements. One of the most important aspects of creating useful observation data is to objectively record behavior you've observed. When recordings are accurate, there's less opportunity for misinterpretation. Alternatively, you might videotape the program, which has some advantages. All the stakeholders, including those who are videotaped, can conduct the observation evaluation. A videotape provides a permanent record that can be repeatedly analyzed. Whereas questionnaires and surveys can probe opinions and perceptions, observations provide evidence that a program is effective.

Interviews

Interviewing takes practice. The beauty of an interview is that you can discuss in depth the perspective of a stakeholder and take time to get clarification on any or all aspects of the evaluation. Questions must be carefully designed so that the respondent isn't prompted to give a preferred answer in his or her response. Questions should be pretested to ensure they're clear and easy to interpret. A permanent record of the interview can be made with a tape recorder or video camera.

Journals

In a journal (similar to the personal journal you're completing in this book), stakeholders in the program are encouraged to record their observations, opinions, feelings, and reflections about the program. Most useful is a journal that documents ongoing delivery of the program. Keeping a journal can be a big commitment for stakeholders to make, but the prospect of additional entries in their journals by staff, volunteers, or practicum students might motivate them to consistently complete their postsession journal entries.

The qualitative information retrieved from questionnaires, observations, interviews, and journals should be evaluated in terms of improving program effectiveness. This means viewing it in terms both of the individual participant and the program overall. Information (data) that appears consistently can be used to instigate program change, whereas information that's participant specific can be used to help accommodate the unique needs of that person. It's important to have several stakeholders review the data and discuss their findings. This is a time-consuming process that can be difficult when it comes to agreeing on the interpretation of the data. As a practicum student, you might not participate in this process because it could occur after you've left your placement.

Summary

Understanding evaluation processes helps you improve programs. Creating a program evaluation that's person-centered is essential to becoming a practitioner who can meet individual needs. Understanding your values, attitudes, and beliefs about disability plays a large part in this task.

Exercise 9.1
Global Program Evaluation

As much as possible, this evaluation should include the views and opinions of participants in the program, their family or significant others, the administrators and supervisors of the program, and, of course, your perspective as a practicum student. If you're permitted to administer a questionnaire at your practicum site, you can adapt the following sample to suit your needs. Include as many stakeholders as possible. If you don't have permission to administer a questionnaire in the program, complete it for yourself as a stakeholder. If you're given an evaluation tool designed for your practicum site, ask for permission to use it to evaluate another stakeholder. Take advantage of this opportunity to learn more about the effect of the program. You might encounter a few surprises—you never know.

Sample Program Evaluation

(Note: All confidentiality and information privacy laws must be addressed before an evaluation can be administered in a program or with participants.)

Name of program: _____

People served by the program: _____

Respondent (e.g., participant, instructor, parent, practicum student): _____

Please respond to the following statements by indicating your agreement or disagreement. Following each statement is a space available for you to comment on your response.

Part 1: Program Design

1. The goals and objectives of the program are clear.

Strongly agree   Agree   Don't know   Don't agree   Strongly disagree

_____

_____

2. The number of sessions per week of program delivery, which is _____, is just right.

Strongly agree   Agree   Don't know   Don't agree   Strongly disagree

_____

_____

3. Time duration for each session is just right.

Strongly agree   Agree   Don't know   Don't agree   Strongly disagree

_____

_____

4. The time of day for these sessions is just right.

Strongly agree   Agree   Don't know   Don't agree   Strongly disagree

_____

_____

5. Suitable written policies and procedures guide the operations of the program.

Strongly agree   Agree   Don't know   Don't agree   Strongly disagree

_____

_____

6. Orientation is provided to all program participants.

Strongly agree   Agree   Don't know   Don't agree   Strongly disagree

_____

_____

7. Orientation is required of practicum students.

Strongly agree   Agree   Don't know   Don't agree   Strongly disagree

_____

_____

8. Preprogram screening or testing is always conducted.

Strongly agree   Agree   Don't know   Don't agree   Strongly disagree

_____

_____

9. Instructor–student ratio in the program is just right. (Here the term "instructor" refers to practicum students, volunteers, teachers, instructors, supervisors, and anyone else actively working with the participants.)

Strongly agree   Agree   Don't know   Don't agree   Strongly disagree

_____

_____

10. Program supervisor or administrator presence is appropriate; there is someone constantly available to offer assistance and guidance.

Strongly agree   Agree   Don't know   Don't agree   Strongly disagree

_____

_____

11. There is high compatibility between the program and its location.

Strongly agree   Agree   Don't know   Don't agree   Strongly disagree

_____

_____

12. The equipment available is suitable.

Strongly agree   Agree   Don't know   Don't agree   Strongly disagree

_____

_____

13. Transportation of participants to and from the programs is appropriate.

Strongly agree   Agree   Don't know   Don't agree   Strongly disagree

_____

_____

14. The program promotes interaction among individuals.

Strongly agree   Agree   Don't know   Don't agree   Strongly disagree

_____

_____

15. The program uses appropriately qualified personnel.

Strongly agree   Agree   Don't know   Don't agree   Strongly disagree

_____

_____

16. The program's effectiveness is evaluated regularly.

Strongly agree   Agree   Don't know   Don't agree   Strongly disagree

_____

_____

17. The environmental assessment (see chapter 7) revealed the following recommended changes.

_____

_____

_____

Part 2: Program Content

18. The program's content reflects the goals of the program.

Strongly agree   Agree   Don't know   Don't agree   Strongly disagree

_____

_____

19. Program activities are age appropriate.

Strongly agree   Agree   Don't know   Don't agree   Strongly disagree

_____

_____

20. The program offers adequate options or accommodations.

Strongly agree   Agree   Don't know   Don't agree   Strongly disagree

_____

_____

21. Program activities motivate me to be more active.

Strongly agree   Agree   Don't know   Don't agree   Strongly disagree

_____

_____

22. There's adequate variety from session to session.

Strongly agree   Agree   Don't know   Don't agree   Strongly disagree

_____

_____

Exercise 9.2
Constructive Review

1. What are the participants' strengths relative to this program?

    a. Cognitive

_____

_____

_____

_____

    b. Psychomotor

_____

_____

_____

_____

    c. Affective

_____

_____

_____

_____

TIP Chapter 6 on learning plans explains the cognitive, psychomotor, and affective domains.

2. These are the learner's program objectives, which you have created together:

_____

_____

_____

_____

3. Evidence that objectives have been achieved:

_____

_____

_____

_____

10
Leaving Your Practicum

"Disability is not a 'brave struggle' or 'courage in the face of adversity' . . . disability is an art. It's an ingenious way to live."

Neil Marcus

I hugged V and said good-bye, but she was unresponsive. I was somewhat disappointed to end the sessions on this note, but I accept the fact, and I know deep down that V enjoyed my company (most of the time), and our time together did result in a positive progression on behalf of V and myself. —Michelle B. (Connelly, 1994, p. 321)

Like most things in life, your practicum is time limited, and leaving your practicum is inevitable. Until now you probably haven't thought much about it. The end of your practicum will likely coincide with the end of your semester—a busy time for you. However, this juncture is an important part of the practicum experience. There might be tasks or responsibilities for you to complete to conclude your practicum. There's much for you to consider as you prepare to bring closure to this chapter in your learning journey.

Leaving the Participants

If you were working with the same person for most or all of your sessions, you might have developed a friendship or sense of companionship with that person, which makes it tough to say good-bye. Working with a group can also result in new friendships. In any case, it's important that you remind your learners in advance that you'll be leaving soon. Sometimes they won't be prepared to hear the news. If you anticipate a particularly tough or unusual good-bye, speak with your supervisor about the best way to handle it. You were urged in chapter 1 to inform your learners that your placement was only temporary. Now is the time to remind them. Also remind them what you have accomplished together and review how they will continue to receive support in their program. Be ready for a range of reactions from the person or people you've come to know. Be prepared with your answer if someone suggests that you see each other again in the future. Your goal is to create a smooth transition for everyone. Just as you sought positive and constructive feedback and support from your supervisor,

Saying good-bye to your new friends can be challenging. By focusing on accomplishments and the things for your learner to continue working on, you'll leave on a positive note and should feel good about it.

your learners need the same from you now. By focusing on accomplishments and the things for your learner to continue working on, you'll leave on a positive note and should feel good about it.

Leaving the Supervisor

Your practicum supervisor has likely been one of the strongest influences on your learning during your practicum. From this person you have learned many things. Review your relationship with your supervisor, and consider the many things you've learned from him or her. There could have been times when you didn't agree; if there's a lingering sense that an issue remains unresolved, now's the time to bring it to closure.

If you have an exit interview, arrive prepared to discuss accomplishments, learning, what went right, what went wrong, and any unresolved issues. If there's no formally scheduled interview, you owe it to your supervisor to arrange a time to have a departure discussion. Your supervisor will have other practicum students in the future, so he or she will benefit from hearing your ideas, opinions, or concerns about the program.

Frequently, a practicum supervisor is responsible for grading your performance. If so, don't leave your last meeting without understanding how your grade was established. This last meeting is also a time to request other evaluative comments he or she might want to share. Most important, ensure an amicable position between you before your practicum terminates. As you leave, thank your supervisor; if you're so inclined, also leave behind a note of thanks.

Leaving the Setting

As you're preparing to leave the practicum setting, consider all the people who have been part of your experience. Acknowledge them on your departure. Thank them and recognize them for the roles they played in your practicum. In many cases, this won't be good-bye forever. If you're in a school or institution, you might be placed there again in the future; if you're at an agency or a center, you might have occasion to visit in the future. Remember that your practicum setting might be the site of your future employment. Leave on good terms with everyone, acknowledging those who helped you with a thank-you note.

This is also a time to consider the nature of your practicum's setting. What did you learn from your assessments and your evaluation? Do your findings support your feelings about the setting? Is it an inviting place that's open and supportive for people with disability? What was the physical setting like as a work environment? How about as an accessible facility for people with disability? In what way, and with what success, did the management and administrative structure function in the program? Were the programs that didn't include people with disability any different? If so, how do you feel about the differences? Were there internal politics that interfered with your program? Your answers to these questions might influence your future career choices. We hope your experience in your practicum will make you more aware of the cultural, psychosocial, and physical environments that you'll work in when your career is established.

Lessons Learned

At the end of your journal, write down what you've learned from your practicum. Lessons learned usually focus on what worked and what didn't work, what went well, and so on. Also review revelations or insights that evolved from your experience. To help you become more aware of yourself as a practitioner and to review your learning outcomes, review your journal and write down the lessons you've learned.

Final Review

At the beginning you recorded goals for your practicum and planned objectives for yourself and your learner(s). Now, in concluding your practicum, your last step is to conduct a final review. In chapter 8 you reviewed your participation in the practicum. You learned that it's important to be honest with yourself without being overly critical. Recall that you were on a learning journey, so your accomplishments outside of your goals and objectives are important as well. In your evaluative review, reflect on how close you came to achieving your goals and objectives. Consider the factors that influenced your work and how they affected the outcomes. Now consider the unplanned outcomes and the conditions under which they evolved. Think about the contribution that all the outcomes made to your practicum experience. Finally, take a personal perspective on your contribution. Evaluate your own performance over the duration of the placement. What personal strengths emerged? How can you build on them? What can you improve on? How?

Recommendations

Programs and schools that host practicum students are usually flexible and open to change. In the words of the business world, they often are "learning organizations." You learn from them, and they learn from you. Part of your growth as a learner is to be able to evaluate and judge (see chapter 6, Bloom's taxonomy). As your part of the leaving exercise, take time to reflect on the organization and the way that it provides service. What are the organization's strengths? In what areas does it need improvement? What things could be changed to improve operations? Take time to consider what you valued and learned the most from. Think about your recommendations for improving the program. At the end of this chapter, you'll be asked to write down your suggestions for improvement. Begin by identifying areas you feel are the strongest features. If appropriate, suggest ways to further improve these areas. Next, consider those areas that in your view didn't work so well; recommend changes in a constructive way.

The Next Practicum

Now that this practicum has concluded, you can begin to cast your eye to the next one. You have determined what lessons you've learned, completed a self-evaluation, considered recommendations, and offered ideas and opinions to your supervisor. Now's the appropriate time to look ahead. In anticipation of a new practicum placement, there's much you can draw on from your previous experience. We suggest creating an inventory of what you can bring to a future placement; in this list, include your strengths, the ways you've changed, lessons you've learned to take to the next practicum, and your aspirations for your next placement.

Rewards of Practicum Placements

The rewards of a practicum can unfold in many ways. Your personal experience might lead to a greater awareness of self and a new appreciation of inclusion as a concept of humanity in society. We hope you enjoyed your experience and made a new friend or two. We know that your practicum must have been challenging, especially at first. Perhaps you were apprehensive about working in a program that you might not have considered were it not a requirement for a course. Overcoming these apprehensions and growing with the practicum is a common reward for practicum students. We hope your practicum experience has made a positive impact on your life.

Work in practica enhances your professional preparation in many ways. You might have developed new contacts in the field and expanded your professional network. You might have worked in a facility that was new to your experience or worked with a professional from a discipline you had never encountered before (e.g., occupational therapist). Many students increase their employment leads through their work in practica. Others later reflect on how their practicum influenced their professional practice in other fields.

Practicum placements offer mutual benefits for you and the institution in which you were placed. Your interest, energy, and commitment to your practicum site are

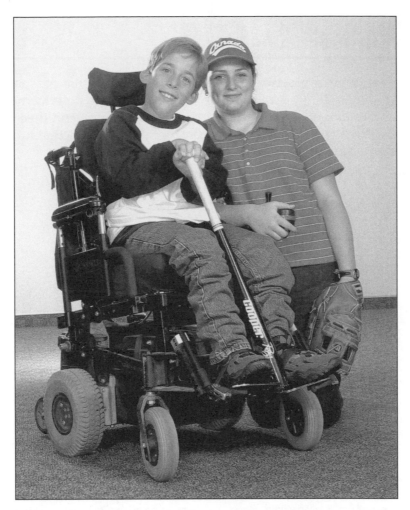

The practicum experience can be rewarding both for you and the learner.

beneficial to them. They learn from you as well. As a preprofessional, you might have brought new ideas and contemporary thinking to their program.

Summary

After taking care of the good-byes and the many final duties you need to fulfill, be sure to take some quiet time for yourself to reflect on your experience in the practicum. These weeks might be the only time in your life you'll work so closely with others—or they might be an introduction to a career in adapted physical activity. Many claim that after leaving their practicum, they miss the rewards the experience presented. If you're feeling a vacant feeling in the weeks and months after your practicum has concluded, consider volunteering in the program or in a similar situation. There are never enough experienced volunteers for APA programs. As trite as it may sound, you *can* make a difference. Likely, you already have.

Reviewing Your Practicum

Begin the review of your practicum experience with a personal perspective of your contribution. Evaluate how successful you consider your own performance over the duration of the placement. Review your goals and objectives, and then reflect on the extent of your achievement in each. Now consider those factors that influenced your work. Write about how they affected the outcomes.

1. Here's how I view my overall contribution:

_____

_____

_____

2. I view my achievement of my goals and objectives as follows:

_____

_____

_____

3. The following factors influenced my work and affected the outcomes of my practicum in the following ways:

_____

_____

_____

_____

4. During the practicum, what personal strengths emerged? How can you build on them? What can you improve on? How?

_____

_____

_____

_____

_____

5. Now consider the unplanned outcomes and the conditions under which they evolved.

_____

_____

_____

_____

_____

Evaluating Your Practicum Supervision

If you were in a supervised practicum, think about your practicum supervisor. If it's appropriate to offer feedback, share your responses to the following questions with your supervisor.

Answer the following questions:

1. What did you observe about your practicum supervisor's approach, teaching (coaching, leading) style, and abilities?
2. Was your practicum supervisor available to you enough?
3. How well did your supervisor communicate with you? Was he or she easy to approach and talk to?
4. How well did your supervisor support your efforts?
5. How well did your supervisor challenge your assumptions or your actions?
6. How much or how often were you encouraged or challenged to be reflective in your practice?
7. To what degree were you given responsibility and self-direction?
8. What's your opinion on your supervisor's knowledge base and ability to integrate knowledge into practice?

Evaluating the Practicum Overall

Circle the answer that best matches your feelings and views.

1. I generally felt prepared when I went to my practicum

1   2   3   4   5

Strongly disagree   Strongly agree

2. I now think more about what and why I'm instructing (or coaching) and how I do it.

1   2   3   4   5

Strongly disagree   Strongly agree

3. I am more aware of my feelings.

1   2   3   4   5

Strongly disagree   Strongly agree

4. I applied course content (my APA course as well as other courses) during my practice.

1   2   3   4   5

Strongly disagree   Strongly agree

5. I am more aware of disability as a social construct.

| 1 | 2 | 3 | 4 | 5 |

Strongly disagree   Strongly agree

6. Comment on what was and what wasn't helpful.

_____

_____

_____

_____

Exercise 10.4
Think Ahead to Your Next Practicum

1. What type of setting would you like to work in? Why?

_____

_____

_____

_____

_____

2. What qualities do you know you can bring to the next practicum? How do you know this? What evidence is there from your practicum? Identify five of your qualities, supporting these with evidence and examples from your practicum.

_____

_____

_____

_____

_____

_____

_____

_____

_____

_____

_____

3. What two personal qualities would you like to moderate in your next practicum? Why are you interested in changing this quality? What else do you think you'll do differently in your next practicum?

_____

_____

_____

_____

_____

TIP Moderating personal qualities means that you want to do less of something.

4. Last chance: any other comments?

_____

_____

_____

_____

_____

APPENDIX

Journal Writing Guidelines

Purpose

The purpose of keeping a journal is to bring together the knowledge you're acquiring in class with the experience of your practicum through a reflective writing process that adds a personal dimension to your learning.

Process

1. Write one entry for each practicum session.
2. Use a separate page for each entry.
3. Date each entry.
4. Underline any course concept or theoretical information related to your practicum experience.
5. Review your entries and assess the following:
   - The depth of thinking
   - The variety of entries (according to suggestions in this manual [pages 31-36])
   - The quality of writing

Tailor your journal to your practicum setting and your personal experience.

Journal

Date: _____

_____

_____

_____

_____

_____

References

Abramson, J. & Fortune, A. (1990). Improving field instruction: An evaluation of a seminar for new field instructors. *Journal of Social Work Education, 26,* 273-286.

Anderson, G. (1999). The living question of school improvement and school effectiveness. *Education Today,* 11(2), 29.

Andrews, J. & Lupart, J. (1993). *The inclusive classroom: Educating exceptional children.* Scarborough, ON: Nelson Canada.

Bandura, A. (1997). *Self-efficacy: The exercise of control.* New York: W.H. Freeman.

Biley, F. & Smith, K. (1998). "The buck stops here": Accepting responsibility for learning and actions after graduation from a problem based learning nursing education curriculum. *Journal of Advanced Nursing,* 27(5), 1021-1029.

Block, M.E. & Conaster, P. (1999). Consulting in adapted physical education. *Adapted Physical Activity Quarterly,* 16(1), 9-26.

Blom, S.D., Lininger, R.S., & Charlesworth, W.R. (1987). Ecological observation of emotionally and behaviorally disordered children: An alternative method. *American Journal of Orthopsychiatry, 57,* 49-59.

Bloom, B.S. (1956). *Taxonomy of educational objectives: Cognitive domain.* New York: David McKay.

Bronfenbrenner, U. (1979). *The ecology of human development.* Cambridge, MA: Harvard University.

Brown, R.I. (1992). Personal communication, December 7.

Bush, P. (1972). *A programmed course for the writing of performance objectives.* Chico, CA: North California Program Development Center.

Coalition for Active Living (2002). *Words with dignity.* disability.alliance@activeliving.ca

Connelly, M. (1994). Practicum experiences and journal writing in adapted physical education: Implications for teacher education. *Adapted Physical Activity Quarterly,* 11, 306-328.

Custer, R. (1994). *Performance based implementation handbook.* University of Missouri, Columbia, MO: Instructional Materials Laboratory.

Custer, R.L., Schell, J., McAlister, B.D., Scott, J.L., & Hoepfl, M. (2000). Using authentic assessment in vocational education (Information Series No. 381). Columbus, OH: ERIC Clearinghouse on Adult, Career, and Vocational Education.

Emes, C. & Legg, D. (2004). Disability sport simulation activities in adapted physical activity: Experiences of participants and persons with a disability. Under review.

Emes, C., Longmuir, P., & Downs, P. (2002). An abilities-based approach to professional service delivery in adapted physical activity. *Adapted Physical Activity Quarterly,* 19(4), 403-419.

Fletcher, V. (2003). Universal design: Human-centered design for the 21st century. Retrieved August 31, 2003 from www.adaptenv.org / index.php?option=Resource&articleid=148& topicid=5.

Franken, R. (1994). *Human motivation.* Pacific Grove, CA: Brooks/Cole.

Galagan, J.E. (1985). Psychoeducational testing: Turn out the lights, the party's over. *Exceptional Children,* 52(3), 288-299.

Gardner, H. (1993). *Multiple intelligences: The theory in practice. A reader.* New York: Basic Books.

Hellison, D., Cutforth, N., Kallusky, J., Martinek, T., Parker, M., & Stiehl, J. (2000). *Youth development and physical activity.* Champaign, IL: Human Kinetics.

Hettich, P.I. (1992). *Learning skills for college and career.* Pacific Grove, CA: Brooks/Cole.

Huitt, W. (2001, April). *Motivation to learn: An overview.* Accessed November 1, 2003, at http://chiron.valdosta.edu/whuitt/col/motivation/motivate.html.

Jeffreys, M. & Gall, R. (1996). *The learning journey.* Calgary: Detselig Enterprises Ltd.

Johnson, L. (1986). Factors that influence skill acquisition of practicum students during a field-based experience. *Teacher Education and Special Education, 9*(3), 89-103.

Johnson, L. (1987). The role of the university supervisor: Perceptions of practicum students. *Teacher Education and Special Education, 10*(3), 120-125.

Johnson, P. (1985). The role of the voluntary society in Canada. In Jackson, R. (Ed.), *Wessex studies in special education* (pp. 77-88). Winchester: King Alfred's College.

Kiger, G. (1992). Disability simulations: Logical, methodological and ethical issues. *Disability, Handicap & Society, 7*(1), 71-78.

Knight, C. (2001). The process of field instruction: BSW and MSW students' views of effective field supervision. *Journal of Social Work Education, 37*(2), 357-379.

Kolb, D.A. (1984). *Experiential learning. Experience as the source of learning and development.* Englewood Cliffs, NJ: Prentice-Hall.

Krathwohl, D.R., Bloom, B.S., & Masia, B.B. (1964). *Taxonomy of educational objectives: Affective domain.* New York: David McKay.

LaMaster, K., Kinchin, G., & Siedentop, D. (1999). Inclusion practice of effective elementary specialists. *Adapted Physical Activity Quarterly, 15*(4), 329-344.

Lee, L. (1999). Partners in pedagogy: Collaboration between university and secondary school foreign language teachers (ERIC Digest). Washington, DC: ERIC Clearinghouse on Languages and Linguistics. (ERIC Document Reproduction Service No. ED435186 1999-10-00)

Linert, C., Sherrill, C., & Myers, B. (2001). Physical educators' concerns about integrating children with disabilities: A cross cultural comparison. *Adapted Physical Activity Quarterly, 18*(1), 1-17.

Longmuir, P.E. (2003). Creating inclusive physical activity opportunities: An abilities-based approach. In Steadward, R.D., Wheeler, G.D., & Watkinson, E.J. (Eds.), *Adapted physical activity* (pp. 363-382). Edmonton: The University of Alberta Press.

Lonsdale, S. (1990). *Women and disability.* New York: St. Martin's Press.

Lund, J. (1997). Authentic assessment: Its development and application. *Journal of Physical Education, Recreation & Dance, 68*(7), 25-28, 40.

Lytle, R.K. & Collier, D. (2002). The consultation process: Adapted physical education specialists' perceptions. *Adapted Physical Activity Quarterly, 19*, 261-279.

Lytle, R.K. & Hutchinson, G.E. (2004). Adapted physical educators: The multiple roles of consultants. *Adapted Physical Activity Quarterly, 21*, 34-49.

Michalko, R. (2002). *The difference that disability makes.* Philadelphia: Temple University Press.

O'Brien, C.L. & O'Brien, J. (2000). *The origins of person-centered planning: A community of practice perspective.* Lithonia, GA: Responsive Systems Associates, Inc.

O'Brien, J. (1997). *What is self-determination?* [Video.] Irene M. Ward & Associates.

O'Brien, J. & O'Brien, C.L. (1998). *A little book about person centered planning.* Toronto: Inclusion Press.

Okahashi, P. & Roby-Straza, W. (2002). Positively practical: A case study of a practicum placement. *Rehabilitation Review, 13*(6).

Olkin, R. (1999). *What psychotherapists should know about disability.* New York: The Guilford Press.

Rich, D.C., Robinson, G., & Bednarz, R.S. (2000). Collaboration and the successful use of information and communications technologies in teaching and learning. *Journal of Geography in Higher Education,* 24(2), 263-271.

Rogers, G., Collins, D., Barlow, C., & Grinnell Jr., R. (2000). *Guide to the social work practicum: A team approach.* Itasca, IL: F.E. Peacock.

Rudner, L.M. & Boston, C. (1994). Performance assessment. *The ERIC Review,* 3(1), 2-12.

Ryan, G., Toohey, S., & Hughes, C. (1996). The purpose, value, and structure of the practicum in higher education: A literature review. *Higher Education,* 3(3), 355-377.

Salend, S.J., Johansen, M., Mumper, J., Chase, A.S., Pike, K.M., & Dorney, J.A. (1997). Cooperative teaching: The voices of two teachers. *Remedial and Special Education,* 18(1), 3-11.

Stanovich, P.J. (1996). Collaboration—The key to successful instruction in today's schools. *Intervention in School and Clinic,* 32(1), 39-42.

Stiehl, R. & Bessey, B. (1993). *The green thumb myth: Managing learning in high performance organizations.* Corvallis, OR: The Learning Organization.

Vazquez, A.S. (1977). *The philosophy of praxis.* Atlantic Highlands, NJ: Humanities Press.

Wiggins, G. (1989). A true test: Toward more authentic and equitable assessment. *Phi Delta Kappan,* 69, 703-713.

Winnick, J. (2000). *Adapted physical education and sport* (3rd ed.). Champaign, IL: Human Kinetics.

World Health Organization. (2001). *International classification of functioning, disability and health.* Accessed January 3, 2003, at http://www3.who.int/icf/icftemplate.cfm?myurl=homepage.html&mytitle=Home%20Page.

About the Authors

Claudia Emes, PhD, faculty of kinesiology, the University of Calgary, has been a professor and researcher of adapted physical activity (APA) for many years. She has organized and run Special Olympics competitions and a national paralympic competition, and she wrote a seminal article on the abilities-based approach to APA published in *Adapted Physical Activity Quarterly* in fall of 2002. She has also participated in the creation and delivery of a program of inclusive postsecondary education for people with intellectual disability. Emes is an active volunteer in APA with several national and international organizations, including Special Olympics Canada, the North American Leadership Council of Special Olympics Inc., and the International Federation of Adapted Physical Activity.

Emes has earned a Teaching Excellence award in kinesiology from the University of Calgary and was named a Woman of Distinction by the YWCA of Calgary in 1998. She lives in Calgary with her husband, Allen, and enjoys spending time with her adult children, along with running, skiing, and reading in her leisure time.

Beth P. Velde, PhD, is an associate professor in the department of occupational therapy at East Carolina University. She has been an educator in therapeutic recreation, adapted physical education, rehabilitation studies, occupational therapy, and related fields. As an educator, she is an active researcher and writer, having authored three other books and two book chapters. She received the Dean's Award for Research in 2002 and was named recipient of the 2003 Distinguished Service Award by the Mental Health Association of Pitt County. Velde is on the National Advisory Panel for Evidence-Based Decision-Making and Active Learning Strategies, and she was a coprincipal investigator for the Learn and Serve Grant. She and her husband, Frank, live in Blounts Creek, North Carolina, where she enjoys running, boating, and writing, in addition to her teaching.

You'll find other
outstanding adapted
physical activity resources at

www.HumanKinetics.com

In the U.S. call

1-800-747-4457

Australia..08 8277 1555
Canada 1-800-465-7301
Europe..+44 (0) 113 255 5665
New Zealand.....................................0064 9 448 1207

HUMAN KINETICS
The Information Leader in Physical Activity
P.O. Box 5076 • Champaign, IL 61825-5076 USA